INSTANT KEYBOARD

Charles Segal
Colleen Segal

Cover design and layout: Kayla Glovinski
Music printing: Kevin O'Shaughnessy

© 1974 Segal's Publications, 58 Burg Street, Cape Town, South Africa
© 1987 Segal's Publications, P.O. Box 507, Newton MA 02459
© 2011 Charles Segal Publications, 16 Grace Road, Ste 1, Newton, MA 02459
All rights reserved.

ISBN-13: 978-1463610913
ISBN-10: 1463610912

Can you "justify" the margins?

ABOUT THE AUTHORS

Charles Segal has enjoyed a long and multi-faceted career in the music business in diverse roles as musician, composer, music publisher, producer, and teacher. His many prestigious awards include the equivalent of a Grammy - South African Record Industry (SARI) Award for Song of the Year (in this book). *page 136*

Charles is an amazing teacher. He was trained in mandolin and classical piano performance and composition and attained a teacher's Licentiate from the Trinity College of London. His "INSTANT" series of music tutor books helps guide aspiring musicians quickly and easily through the basics and his private students find themselves playing INSTANTLY at the first lesson.

Charles is the featured artist on over 500 albums. He has worked with many great musicians, such as Bill Evans, Bud Powell, Cy Coleman Dan Hill and Arthur Prysock; he composes and plays "loops" for Hip-Hop artists and is a popular performer at Hollywood events in celebration of awards such as the Oscars, MTV Movie Awards, Teen and Kids Choice. Charles' music spans a myriad of cultures and styles, including Pop, Jazz, Classical, Contemporary, Film score, Ethnic, African, Relaxing and New Age music. He has produced albums with orchestras, pop groups, singers, traditional African groups, and also children's music for his own label and international record companies.
Learn more about Charles by visiting **www.CharlesSegal.com**

Co-writer Colleen met Charles when she was a keyboardist and singer in the trendy pop group, The In-Set. She is a teacher and author, co-composer and producer of eight full-length musicals, short stories, speech tutors and the INSTANT Music tutor series.

ABOUT THIS BOOK:
INSTANT KEYBOARD is a quick and easy introduction to playing the keyboard and to reading music. To contact the authors by emailing info@ **www.CharlesSegal.com**

INTRODUCTION

We wrote **INSTANT KEYBOARD** because we know there's an **easier way for people to learn the keyboard just for fun**. Let's face it: old-fashioned music lessons can be confusing.

So, we sifted through our playing and teaching experience to find the **bare minimum you need to get you started having fun playing your favorite songs, INSTANTLY.**

10 great things about INSTANT KEYBOARD:

(1) **INSTANT KEYBOARD** gets right to the heart of what you need to know to play.

(2) **INSTANT KEYBOARD** lets you play at the very first lesson.

(3) **INSTANT KEYBOARD** gives you so many **choices**:

- You can **start at Chapter 1 and 2** and **learn to play by ear** – something everybody wants, but most teachers don't know.
- Or you can **skip to Chapter 3** and **read music** immediately.
- You can keep your **left hand simple**, with easy single notes.
- Or you can use our secret weapon in Chapter 9: **Easy INSTANT tricks to sound professional**.

(4) You **don't even need a piano** to start **INSTANT KEYBOARD** – you can just tap a rhythm and mime playing on a table.

(5) **INSTANT KEYBOARD** makes the whole process of **reading music painless**, with our **easy, step-by-step** course that lets you in on the **insider tricks**.

(6) **INSTANT KEYBOARD** is bursting with **popular songs – all in the same key!**

(7) **INSTANT KEYBOARD** shows you how **play in a professional way while you sing.**

(8) **INSTANT KEYBOARD** gives you **INSTANT Scale and INSTANT Chord charts** so you can easily play any songs.

(9) The main thing about **INSTANT KEYBOARD** is that it allows you to **play INSTANTLY** and have **fun**, while teaching you **only what absolutely you need to know** about music.

(10) **INSTANT KEYBOARD** is a bridge to other books in this series, like **INSTANT Keyboard II, INSTANT Classics, INSTANT Jazz, INSTANT Songwriting, INSTANT Guitar** and more.

We know you're going to have fun with **INSTANT KEYBOARD**!
Sincerely,

Charles Segal & Colleen Segal

PS: We forgot to tell you the **best thing** about **INSTANT KEYBOARD:** you can **contact us any time with any questions** by going to our **website: www.CharlesSegal.com**

TABLE OF CONTENTS

CHAPTER 1: PLAY BY EAR – INSTANTLY   7

THE 6 STEPS TO PLAYING BY EAR – INSTANTLY
- STEP ONE – GET COORDINATED
- STEP TWO – FINGER AEROBICS
- STEP THREE – GETTING ACQUAINTED WITH SOUND
- STEP FOUR – DEVELOPING MELODIC SENSE
- STEP FIVE – SCALES AND CHORDS
- STEP SIX – PLAY AND SING MAJOR SCALES - INSTANTLY

PLAY BY EAR IN THE KEY OF C MAJOR – INSTANTLY   31
- CLUES THAT A SONG IS IN C MAJOR

LEFT HAND ACCOMPANIMENT   34
- *MARY HAD A LITTLE LAMB*
- CHORDS IN THE LEFT HAND

TWO HAND ACCOMPANIMENT   39
- *BEAUTIFUL BROWN EYES*
- *WHEN THE SAINTS GO MARCHING IN*

CHAPTER 2: GETTING ACQUAINTED WITH THE KEYBOARD   45

THE KEYBOARD DESIGN
NOTE NAMES AND PATTERNS   47

CHAPTER 3: BASICS OF WRITTEN MUSIC   51

MUSICAL NOTES   53
- C HAND POSITION
- DIRECTIONAL READING

SONGS IN THE C FIVE FINGER POSITION   58
- *ODE TO JOY*
- *MERRILY WE ROLL ALONG*
- *LIGHTLY ROW*

THE LEFT HAND   60
- C HAND POSITION
- ADDING A BASS NOTE

CHAPTER 4: PLAYING CHORDS   62

INSTANT CHORDS
MELODIES WITH CHORDS IN THE LEFT HAND   64
- THE F MAJOR CHORD

MELODIES IN FIVE-FINGER POSITIONS   66
- *JINGLE BELLS*
- *WHEN THE SAINTS GO MARCHING IN*

CHAPTER 5: MUSICAL TIMING — 68

RHYTHM
NOTE VALUES — 69
- QUARTER NOTE
- HALF NOTE
- DOTTED HALF NOTE
- WHOLE NOTE
- EIGHTH NOTE
- DOTTED QUARTER NOTE

BARS, MEASURES AND TIME SIGNATURES — 71

CHAPTER 6: MOVING AROUND THE KEYBOARD — 81

EXTENDING THE C FIVE FINGER POSITION
- *MARY-ANNE*
- *TWINKLE TWINKLE*
- *ON TOP OF OLD SMOKEY*
- *AULD LANG SYNE*

INVERSIONS — 87
- *BRAHMS LULLABY*
- *SILENT NIGHT*
- *BATTLE HYMN OF THE REPUBLIC*

SHARPS, FLATS AND NATURALS — 93
- *FRANKIE AND JOHNNY*

CHAPTER 7: CHORDS — 96

MAJOR AND MINOR — 97
- *STAR SPANGLED BANNER*
- *YELLOW ROSE OF TEXAS*
- *CARELESS LOVE*
- *AMAZING GRACE*
- *HAVA NAGILAH*

PLAYING SCALES FOR FINGER EXERCISE — 104
- *YANKEE DOODLE DANDY*
- *SHE'LL BE COMIN' ROUND THE MOUNTAIN*
- *AMERICA THE BEAUTIFUL*

CHAPTER 8: MORE SIGNS AND SYMBOLS — 108

REPEAT SIGNS AND ENDINGS
RESTS — 110
- *FUR ELISE*
- *MOZART'S SONATA NO. 15*
- *BLUE DANUBE*
- *AURA LEE*
- *RED RIVER VALLEY*
- *HOME ON THE RANGE*
- *THE OLD FOLKS AT HOME*

6/8 TIME SIGNATURE — 116
- *HOUSE OF THE RISING SUN*
- *WHEN JOHNNY COMES MARCHING HOME*

CHAPTER 9: LEFT HAND PATTERNS AND TECHNIQUES — 119

READING THE BASS CLEF
ACCOMPANIMENT PATTERNS — 122
    EXAMPLES
        DEMO ARRANGEMENT – *FRANKIE AND JOHNNY*
        ACCOMPANYING YOUR SINGING
TRANSPOSING ACCOMPANIMENT PATTERNS — 130

BONUS SECTION: ADDITIONAL SONGS TO PLAY — 133

SONGS FOR ALL OCCASIONS
    HAPPY BIRTHDAY
    FOR HE'S A JOLLY GOOD FELLOW
    WE WISH YOU A MERRY CHRISTMAS
    MY COUNTRY 'TIS OF THEE
    I'VE BEEN WORKING ON THE RAILROAD

CHARLES SEGAL ORIGINAL SONGS — 136
    MY CHILDREN, MY WIFE
    YOU'RE NOT ALONE
    OUT OF THIS WORLD
    JUNGLE ROCK AND ROLL

MUSICAL SCALES — 142
    MAJOR
    NATURAL MINOR
    HARMONIC MINOR
    BLUES

CHORD CHART — 149
CIRCLE OF FIFTHS — 151
CHORD SYMBOLS — 152

CHAPTER 1: PLAY BY EAR INSTANTLY

It is not essential that you learn to play by ear before you learn to read music,
but we think it's an important part of a musical education that should be tried early.

If you prefer to go straight to learning how to read music,
you may skip this chapter and come back to it later.

Playing by ear means that you play a song from memory without having to read the music to know which notes to play. You hear the song in your mind and you can transfer what you hear inside to an external instrument.

STEP ONE: GET COORDINATED - INSTANTLY

Music consists of sounds and the silences between the sounds.
Both sounds and silences have a specific amount of time assigned to them.

Exercise # 1: Tap on Anything

"**Tap**" = Make a sound by tapping on something
"**Hold**" = No sound, but nod your head as you read the word "Hold" silently
| = These are lines to divide the sounds – more about them later

Tap exercises 1 - 4.
Imagine each word in sync with the beat of a clock. Keep the rhythm slow and even.
Give the Taps and Holds the same length of time.

Tap	Tap	Tap	Tap		Hold	Hold	Hold	Hold
Tap	Tap	Tap	Tap		Hold	Hold	Hold	Hold
Tap	Hold	Tap	Hold		Tap	Hold	Tap	Hold
Tap	Hold	Tap	Hold		Tap	Hold	Tap	Hold
Tap	Tap	Tap	Tap		Hold	Hold	Hold	Hold
Tap	Tap	Tap	Tap		Tap	Hold	Hold	Hold

Exercise #2

Tap	Tap	Tap	Tap	Tap	Tap	Tap	Hold
Tap	Tap	Tap	Hold	Tap	Tap	Tap	Hold
Tap	Hold	Tap	Hold	Tap	Hold	Tap	Hold
Tap	Tap	Tap	Tap	Tap	Tap	Tap	Tap
Tap	Tap	Tap	Tap	Hold	Hold	Hold	Hold
Tap	Tap	Tap	Tap	Tap	Hold	Hold	Hold

Exercise #3

Tap	Tap	Tap	Hold	Tap	Tap	Tap	Hold
Tap	Tap	Tap	Tap	Tap	Hold	Hold	Hold
Tap	Tap	Tap	Tap	Tap	Tap	Tap	Tap
Tap	Tap	Tap	Tap	Tap	Hold	Tap	Hold

Tap	Tap	Tap	Hold	Tap	Tap	Tap	Hold
Tap	Tap	Tap	Hold	Tap	Tap	Tap	Hold
Tap	Tap	Tap	Tap	Tap	Tap	Tap	Tap
Tap	Tap	Tap	Tap	Tap	Hold	Hold	Hold

Exercise #4

Tap	Tap	Tap	Tap	Tap	Tap	Tap	Tap	Hold	Hold	Hold	Hold
Tap	Tap	Tap	Tap	Tap	Tap	Tap	Hold	Hold	Tap	Hold	Hold
Tap	Tap	Tap	Tap	Tap	Tap	Tap	Tap	Hold	Hold	Hold	Tap
Tap	Tap	Tap	Tap	Tap	Tap	Tap	Hold	Hold	Hold	Hold	Hold

STEP TWO: FIVE - FINGER AEROBICS

Memorize the FINGER NUMBERS of the RIGHT HAND

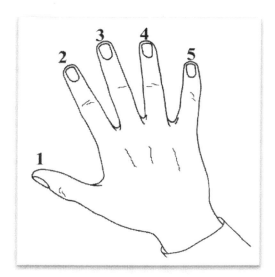

Exercise #5: Using any surface, pretend to be playing the piano

Let the fingers "play" one by one, starting with finger number 1 (the thumb), then going to finger number 2, 3, 4, up to number 5 and then down from finger number 5 to finger number 1. "Play" slowly at first and then faster and faster.

> *TIP:* pick up each finger after you have "played" it, so that there is only one finger down at a time.

Exercise #6: Say the finger numbers aloud as you "play" them

1	2	3	4	5				
5	4	3	2	1				
1	2	3	4	5	4	3	2	1

Exercise #7: Improvise – start with finger number 3 and play in any order,
jumping around at will, making sure you give every finger a chance to "play".

Remember to pick up each finger after you have "played" it.

Say the finger numbers aloud as you "play" them

Exercise #8: "Play" the finger numbers written below.
Remember to always keep a steady rhythm like the second hand on a clock.
Each "Hold" should be given the same length of time as each number.

1	2	3	4	5	Hold	Hold	Hold
5	4	3	2	1	Hold	Hold	Hold

**Do Exercise #8 again, saying aloud the finger numbers and "Holds"
as you play them.**

Exercise #9: "Play" the finger numbers below, keeping a steady rhythm

3	2	1	2	3	3	3	Hold
2	2	2	Hold	3	5	5	Hold
3	2	1	2	3	3	3	3
2	2	3	2	1	Hold	Hold	Hold

Repeat Exercise #9, saying aloud the finger numbers and "Holds" as you play them

TIP: *Play very slowly at first, imagining a slow, even ticking clock.
Increase the speed as you become more proficient.*

Exercise #10: Just like the last song, start with finger number 3

3	3	3	Hold	3	3	3	Hold
3	5	1	2	3	Hold	Hold	Hold
4	4	4	4	4	3	3	3
3	2	2	3	2	Hold	5	Hold
3	3	3	Hold	3	3	3	Hold
3	5	1	2	3	Hold	Hold	Hold
4	4	4	4	4	3	3	3
5	5	4	2	1	Hold	Hold	Hold

"Play" Exercise #10 again. Say the finger numbers and "holds" aloud.

Can you guess what well-known song this is?

Exercise #11: Just like the last song, start with finger number 3.

3	3	3	1	2	3	4	4	Hold	Hold	Hold	Hold
3	3	3	1	2	3	2	Hold	Hold	5	Hold	Hold
3	3	3	1	2	3	4	Hold	Hold	Hold	Hold	5
5	2	3	4	3	2	1	Hold	Hold	Hold	Hold	Hold

"Play" Exercise #11 again, saying the finger numbers and "holds" aloud.

Now that your fingers are limbered up, you are ready to play on a real piano!

STEP THREE: GET ACQUAINTED WITH SOUND

KEY WORDS: *Active Listening – Concentration – Accuracy*

CONQUER YOUR FEARS

It is important that you are comfortable with your instrument. Many people feel so intimidated when confronted with the task of learning a new instrument that they let their fear overcome their desire to play. If music is going to be fun, **you can't be afraid to play or to make mistakes**. The keyboard must be your friend and ally. It is there to serve you and you need to show it who is boss.

Exercise #12:

(i)   Sit in front of the keyboard and PLAY ANY TWO KEYS one after the other with your RIGHT HAND, using TWO DIFFERENT FINGERS.

(ii) Then PLAY ANY TWO KEYS one after the other with your LEFT HAND, using TWO DIFFERENT FINGERS.

(iii) Keep repeating this exercise. SELECT ANY KEYS and CHANGE THE WAY YOU PLAY the notes. For example, play loud and soft, in a different order, or fast and slow. Have fun – there's no wrong way to do this.

(iv) Now do the same PLAYING THREE DIFFERENT KEYS IN EACH HAND, varying the rhythm, playing the Question and Answer game. Play only one note at a time and use different fingers to play the different keys.

(v)   Continue the Q and A game PLAYING FOUR DIFFERENT KEYS IN EACH HAND – it doesn't matter if you jump around or play the keys right next to each other. Have fun with creating your own music.

(vi) Now do the same, PLAYING FIVE DIFFERENT KEYS IN EACH HAND.

Did you notice how although the keys look similar – the sounds they make are different?

The sounds may be high or low, depending on whether you play the right side keys or the left side keys.

When you play the keys going up towards the RIGHT SIDE OF THE KEYBOARD, the notes sound a HIGHER pitch.

When you play the keys going down to the LEFT the notes sound a LOWER pitch.

ACCURATE LISTENING is important when playing by ear.

Some people are born with "a good ear" or "perfect pitch". This means that they know the pitch name of any musical sound they hear without looking at an instrument or music. Most people don't have "perfect pitch". Never fear if you fall into the latter category.

A "good ear" can be developed through ear training...

Here's how:

1. You train your ear to **accurately hear** the pitch of a note.
2. Then you train your voice and ear to **accurately sing the notes you play**.
3. Next, you can move on to being able to **play the notes you sing**, which is the secret to playing by ear.

Your VOICE is the best instrument to perform the sounds that you hear in your mind when you are playing by ear.

> **<u>Note</u>:** *some people's voices don't have a big range. They are limited to singing either lower or higher notes, but cannot do both. If this is the case with you, you need to practice* **pitching a difficult note more quietly** *or in a more comfortable range. For these first exercises, you should* **choose notes that are comfortably within your vocal range***.*

Exercise #13: Listen to the music

There is an important **difference between hearing and listening**.
We hear all kinds of sounds around us every minute of the day, but we ignore most of them. For playing the keyboard we need to **focus all of our attention on listening** to the musical sounds we make.

(i) Sit in front of a keyboard and **STRIKE ANY WHITE** key.

If you have a regular piano, hold the key down until the sound fades away.
If you have an electronic keyboard where the sound fades immediately play the key a few times over.

Notice that keys on the right sound at a higher pitch and keys on the left sound at a lower pitch.

Listen intently to the sound you produce, focusing on the tone, the way it fades and the way it feels to hear it. **Savor** every moment. **Immerse** yourself in the sounds. **Absorb** as much of the soul of the sound as you can. Do not rush.

(ii) When you feel that you have registered the sound in your brain and through your entire being, **STRIKE ANOTHER KEY** - any key - and repeat the whole exercise.

(iii)   **REPEAT THIS EXERCISE on at least 3 MORE KEYS**.
It doesn't matter if you play high sounds or low sounds. Act instinctively.
Try not to consciously choose different keys.

Exercise #14: Sing what you play

(i)   **STRIKE ANY WHITE KEY** in the middle section of the Keyboard.
We will call this note #1.

LISTEN to it for a few seconds, then **SING THE NOTE** that sounds.
Make sure that the note is at a comfortable pitch for you to sing.

> *TIP:* *You can pick a word or a sound to sing. We recommend the "nah" sound as it is the most open and relaxed vowel sound and the "N" is an easy consonant to produce.*

(ii)   Now play the white key immediately **TO THE RIGHT** of note #1.
We will call this note #2.

LISTEN to it for a few seconds, then **SING THE NOTE** that sounds.

(iii)   Play the two notes in random order, **making your own melody**.

For example, play **1 2 - 1 2 - 1 1 - 2 2 - 1 2 - 1 1 - 2 1 - 2 1 - 1 2 - 2 1**

(iv)   Keep making your melody on these two keys, but this time, **SING THE NOTES YOU PLAY**.

Concentrate on making your voice sing the exact pitch of the notes you play.
At first you will play a note, and then sing it.
Eventually you should be able to sing the note at the same time you play it.

Exercise #15: Play What You Sing

The next step is to continue with the same two-note melody, but this time, **the only sound should come from your voice**.
Now you have to remember what the two notes sound like without playing them first.

Sing notes 1 and 2 from Exercise #14.

Mime playing the notes on the keyboard as you sing them. Touch the keys lightly, but do not press down to sound the note. The only sound should be your voice.

Every once in a while you should test yourself to make sure that you are singing the pitch accurately by pressing down and sounding the key after you sing the note.

Exercise #16: Adding a New Note

Once you feel confident, you may **ADD AN EXTRA NOTE**, either one key up or one key down from your original two keys.

Now MAKE A MELODY OF THREE NOTES, repeating the whole process:

1. LISTEN to the sound of the notes you play.

2. SING what you play.

3. PLAY what you sing.

> ***TIP:*** *It is easier to have your melodies playing notes in steps – keys right next to each other. Once you gain more confidence, you could add skips – that is, leaving out a key and going to the next one up or down.*

Exercise #17: Challenge

Once you feel confident singing 3 note melodies, you can continue adding as many notes as you wish.

STEP 4: DEVELOP MELODIC SENSE

When we play by ear, we repeat a song or melody that we have heard before, so, if you have a sense of how melodies are formed, you can more easily play by ear.

Melodies move from one note to another in a series of STEPS, SKIPS or JUMPS.

The following simple exercises will introduce your ear to a wealth of musical sounds, including ALL THE NOTES YOU NEED TO PLAY A MELODY IN THE KEY OF C MAJOR, which uses only the white keys. We will explain more about keys later.

WHICH FINGERS TO USE:

You may choose to use any fingers to play the exercises or you can follow our fingering suggestions to advance your musical experience.

Exercise #18: Play a Melody With Your RIGHT HAND

Use fingers 1, 2, and 3 in the following order: **3   2   1   2   3   3   3**

WHERE TO START ON THE KEYBOARD:

Picture 1.1 shows you your starting position.

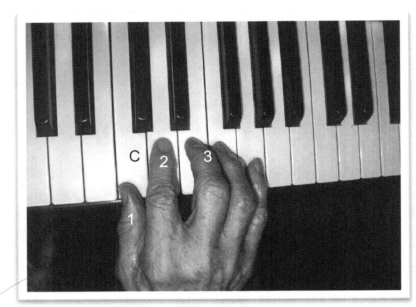

Picture 1.1

(i) Place fingers 1, 2 and 3 in the positions numbered on the diagram.

This is the <u>C five-finger position</u>.

Play the keys under the numbered fingers in this order: **3   2   1   2   3   3   3**

Repeat three or more times until you get used to the melody.

(ii) Now, repeating the same melody pattern, **SING WHAT YOU PLAY**.
Listen carefully to be sure that you are matching your voice to the note.
Repeat at least three times.

(iii) Repeat the same melody, but **PLAY WHAT YOU SING**.

Remember, you **mime playing the keys while you sing the notes** that would sound if you played the keys.

Check yourself every now and then to make sure you are singing the correct pitch.

Repeat this three times.

Exercise #19: Expanding the Melody

Once you feel confident and have absorbed this melody, **MOVE THE MELODIC PATTERN TO THE RIGHT BY ONE WHITE KEY**.

(i) Keep the same finger positions and move your fingers one white key to the right. Check your position in Picture 1.2

Picture 1.2

PLAY THE MELODY: 3 2 1 2 3 3 3

You will notice that, although you are playing the same finger numbers and the same melodic pattern, the melody sounds different.
By starting on the next note up, you are now playing in a different key – a minor key, which has a sadder sound than the first melody, which was in a major key. You'll learn more about major and minor keys later.

Now **SING WHAT YOU PLAY** – be careful – this melody is different!

Then **PLAY WHAT YOU SING.**

(ii) **REPEAT** this exercise with the same pattern going up the keyboard **one key to the right.**

Copy the three finger positions pictured in Pictures 1.3 – 1.5 on the next page.

In each of the three positions, you **PLAY THE PATTERN, SING WHAT YOU PLAY**, then **MIME PLAYING WHILE YOU SING**.

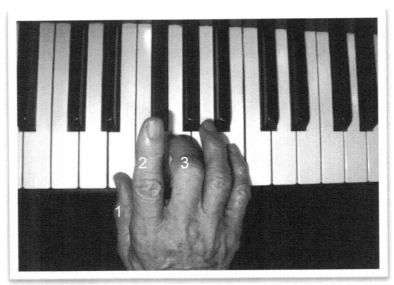
Picture 1.3

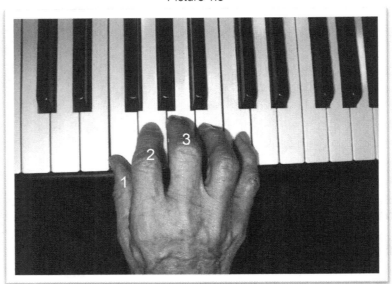
Picture 1.4

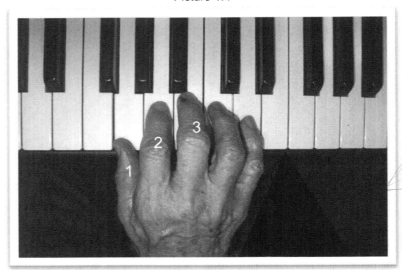
Picture 1.5

(iii) **Return to the beginning, one key at a time.**

    Repeat the last exercise, playing: **3 2 1 2 3 3 3**

You will be moving the pattern one white key to the left each time, repeating the melody going downwards, until you finish back at the first position shown in picture 1.1.

In each of the five positions, you **PLAY THE PATTERN, SING WHAT YOU PLAY**, then **MIME PLAYING WHILE YOU SING**.

STEP 5: DEVELOP A SENSE OF SCALES AND CHORDS

SCALES and CHORDS are two of the most important tools in playing music.

The **scale is the foundation on which melodies and chords are built**.
It is important for your ears to become very well acquainted with what scales sound like.

DEFINITIONS:

PITCH is the sound of a note – low or high

INCREASING PITCH = going higher

DECREASING PITCH = going lower

A **SCALE** is a series of notes of increasing or decreasing pitch arranged within one octave.

An **OCTAVE** is the distance between notes of the same name – there are 8 notes in an octave.

8ve = a shorthand way to write "Octave".

A **CHORD** is a set of 3 or more notes of a scale played simultaneously.

A **PHRASE** is a series of notes in a Melody.

Exercise #20: The Chromatic Scale

The Chromatic Scale is the **easiest scale** to begin with, because you simply play every key, both black and white, in the order it appears on the keyboard.

Like most scales, you **begin and end on the same letter key**, an octave higher or lower than where you started.

You play **thirteen keys** in a Chromatic Scale.

The best thing about the Chromatic Scale is that **once you know one, you know them all**.

Which Fingers to Use:

Use only three fingers to play a Chromatic Scale - the first (thumb), second and third fingers. (Let your fourth and fifth fingers take a vacation for now).

Playing the Chromatic Scale is easy if you remember that **the third finger is the only finger to play the black keys**.

The **first and second fingers play the white keys**.

Playing a Chromatic scale, and knowing the correct fingering, will help train you to use the most convenient fingers when playing any song.

The diagram below shows the whole **C Chromatic Scale** with the finger numbers written over the keys.

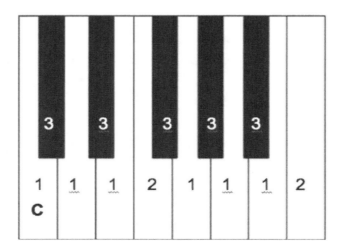

SUMMARY OF HOW TO PLAY THE C CHROMATIC SCALE:

(i) Put your **first finger** on the white key to the left of the group of 2 black keys in the middle section of the keyboard. Play that note – it's called **Middle C**.

(ii) Next, with your **third finger**, play the black key to the immediate right of that key (C#).

(iii) Then tuck your thumb under and play the next white key up (D) and then the next black key with your third finger (D#).

(iv) Tuck your thumb under again and play the next white key up (E).

(v) Now you'll notice that there are two white keys next to each other, so do the natural thing – play the next white key (F) with your second finger! And that leads you on to playing the next black key up (F#) with your third finger, and so on.

(vi) When you get back to the same key you started on, one octave higher (C), you will play that with your second finger and then go back down again, playing the next key down (B) with your first finger.

(vii) Now you have a black key lower than your first finger, so you simply swing your third finger over your thumb to the left, and play that black key (Bb).

(viii) You continue in this way, playing the black keys with the third finger, the whites with the first, until you come to the end of the group of 3 black keys. You play that last black key (F#) with the third finger and then the next white key to the left (F) is played with the second finger so that the thumb is free to play the following white key (E).

(ix) Continue downwards using only the third finger for the black notes until you reach the same note you began with – Middle C.

Once you get the knack of playing the C Chromatic Scale using the correct fingering, you can try starting a Chromatic Scale on any other key and playing an octave up and down.

Congratulations! You've just learned your first scale! That wasn't so bad, was it?

Exercise #21: LISTEN, PLAY AND SING

Practice your ear-training exercises using parts or all of the notes in a Chromatic Scale.

Remember to always: **LISTEN CAREFULLY**
SING WHAT YOU PLAY
PLAY WHAT YOU SING

Exercise #22: Scales and Chords – Five Notes at a Time

In the following exercise, you will be using ALL FIVE FINGERS OF EACH HAND.

(i)   **Place your right hand** on the keyboard in the position shown in **Picture 1.6**

Picture 1.6

Press down and play the keys under the following fingers slowly and firmly:

1 - 2 - 3 - 4 - 5 - 3 - 1

Listen to the notes you play.
Notice that the melody pattern includes steps and skips.

SCALE NOTES = Going up in steps you play all 5 keys next to each other under your 5 fingers. Make sure you lift your finger up off the keys after playing each note so that the sound does not run together with the next note.

CHORD NOTES = Going up, you skip fingers 2 and 4, playing only fingers **5 – 3 – 1** which form a C major CHORD.

(ii) **SING EACH NOTE** carefully and accurately as you play.
Keep repeating this until you have the phrase embedded in your mind.

(iii) Now **SING THE PHRASE FROM MEMORY, MIMING** that you are playing the phrase. Repeat this until you are confident that you are singing accurately. Remember to periodically check by playing the notes.

(iv) **PLAY THE SAME PHRASE AGAIN**:
This time, when you are playing the descending notes (fingers 5 3 1), **DON'T RELEASE the KEYS** after you play them, so that the sounds of the keys under fingers 5, 3 and 1 melt together in a pleasant sounding C Major **CHORD.** Once you feel confident in your playing, you may SING the phrase again with your piano playing as accompaniment.

(v) **MOVE UP ONE KEY:**
When you are able to sing and play this phrase accurately without any mistakes, keeping in that same 5-finger position, **move your hand to the right by one white key.** See the hand position in Picture 1.7. **Play the same phrase again, this time in a higher key** using the same fingers: **1 - 2 - 3 - 4 - 5 - 3 - 1**

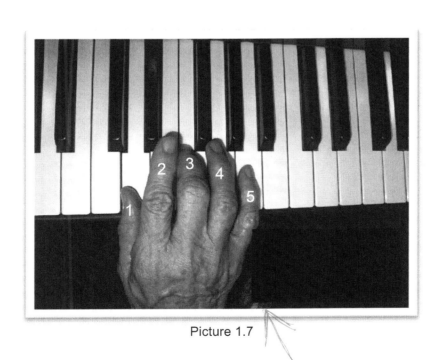

Picture 1.7

(vi) **Go through Steps (i) – (iv) in this new position.**
Concentrate carefully, making sure that you **LISTEN** to the subtle difference in this minor key and that your voice accurately **SINGS** the new phrase.
Don't forget to **hold down the descending three notes** to form a minor chord.

© 2011 Charles Segal Publications, 16 Grace Rd. Ste 1, Newton, MA 02459

(vii) **MOVE your hand position UP ONE KEY** to the next set of white keys.
Go back through Steps (i) – (iv) in the new position shown in Picture 1.8.

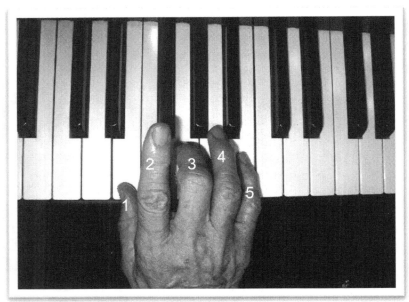

Picture 1.8

(viii) **Continue this exercise, moving up one white key at a time** repeating steps (i) – (iv) until you reach the same key that you started on (C), one octave higher.

> **Note:** *As you go towards the right hand side of the keyboard, the notes will sound progressively higher and may become too difficult to sing. In this case, either try singing the exact note, very softly in a Falsetto voice, or sing the same pitch an octave lower.*

Exercise #23: Left Hand Practice

When you play by ear, either to perform or accompany yourself while singing, ideally you will be playing the keyboard with both hands to give a fuller sound.

The following exercises will give your ear an opportunity to hear the scale and chords in a lower register.

(i) Place your left hand on the keyboard in the position shown below. Note that you will be placing your pinkie finger (5) on C an octave below middle C.

Picture 1.9

Play fingers: **5 - 4 - 3 - 2 - 1 - 3 - 5**

Remember to release the keys as you play, so only one note sounds at a time.

Hold down fingers 1, 3 and 5 on the way down to play a C Major CHORD.

> **Note:** *If you are right-handed, these exercises for the left hand will feel more awkward to play. This is natural – it will become easier the more you practice. Just play slowly and carefully until you become more comfortable with the left hand.*

(ii) Go back to Exercise #22 and play steps (i) – (vii) with your left hand, starting with finger 5 of your left hand on the C an octave below middle C (Picture 1.9). Concentrate well and try your best to accurately sing as many low notes as are comfortable.

> **Note:** *The low notes may be difficult for you to pitch exactly. If this is the case, either try singing the note very softly, or pitch the same note an octave higher.*

BONUS PAGE

To help you become more proficient, you may extend your ear training and hand coordination exercise program by completing the bonus exercises on this page.

Or you can **Move on to STEP 6** and come back to this bonus page later, when you feel like a challenge.

BONUS EXERCISE: DO THE EXERCISES BACKWARDS

Repeat the concept of five scale notes and a chord, but this time go backwards, starting with the highest note.

Remember to play the notes, sing what you play, then play what you sing.

RIGHT HAND:

Begin where the last right hand exercise ended in the **C five-finger position.**
Place your first finger (thumb) on the C **above middle C.**

Play these fingers: **5 - 4 - 3 - 2 - 1 - 3 - 5**

Continue the exercise repeating the same pattern, **moving your hand position one key to the left each time** until you get back to your original hand position with your **first finger on Middle C**.

LEFT HAND:

Begin in the C five-finger position with finger number 5 on the C an octave below Middle C.

Now play these fingers: **1 - 2 - 3 - 4 - 5 - 3 - 1**

Continue the exercise repeating the same pattern, **moving your hand position one key to the left each time** until you return to the C five-finger position, 2 octaves below Middle C.

PRACTICE CHALLENGE:

If you *really* want to improve your playing, you may try to **play the left and right hands together**, simultaneously.

STEP 6: PLAY AND SING MAJOR SCALES - INSTANTLY

To finish your initial ear training, you should learn **the sound of a major scale**, since it is probably the scale most commonly used to write songs. If you know the notes used to write a song, it will be much easier to play that song by ear.

All major scales sound alike because they have the same tonal pattern.

The only difference between the major scales is that they start on different notes.
So, **once you know the sound of the C major scale, you will know what all major scales sound like**.

A basic (diatonic) scale is **one octave** (eight notes), in length.

You **begin and end on the same letter note** an octave higher or lower than the one on which you started.

Exercise #24

You may use any fingering you like to play a scale, but if you want to master the technique of playing your instrument, you should use the fingering as instructed.

Because a scale has eight notes, you should use special fingering to play a scale comfortably.

It's simple math – **3 fingers + 5 fingers** = 8 keys in a scale

The order of the fingers in many scales is: **1 2 3 - 1 2 3 4 5**

And in reverse: **5 4 3 2 1 - 3 2 1**

move to next page

PLAYING THE C MAJOR SCALE WITH THE RIGHT HAND

(i) Place your right hand in the position shown in Picture 1.10

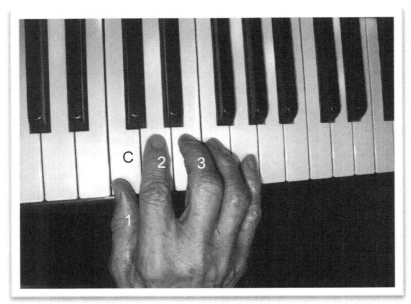

Picture 1.10

The first finger plays the white key to the left of the group of 2 black keys. This is called Middle C.

Play the first three fingers: 1 2 3

After you have played the third finger, the **next key up is played with the first finger** again.

Just tuck your thumb under your third finger and press down the next key to the right. You already had practice doing this in the exercises on the Chromatic Scale.

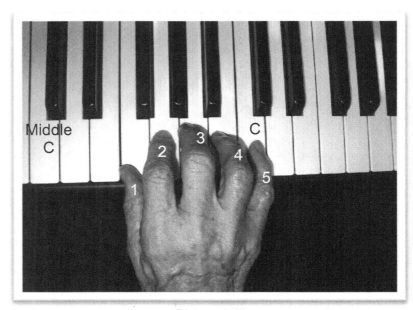

Picture 1.11

When you reach the 8th key with your fifth finger, **proceed back down the scale again**, playing fingers: **4 3 2 1**

After you have played the first finger, **switch back to the third finger** to play the next white key to the left.

You have just played the C Major Scale!

Practice playing the C Major Scale several times until you can do it smoothly.

(ii) Now play the same scale again, **singing** what you play.

Continue playing and singing this scale three or more times until you have its sound firmly fixed in your ear and brain.

(iii) Now try **singing the scale without playing** it. Don't forget to check yourself by playing the note you are singing every now and then.

PLAYING THE C MAJOR SCALE WITH THE LEFT HAND

(i) Place your **left hand** in the position shown in Picture 1.12

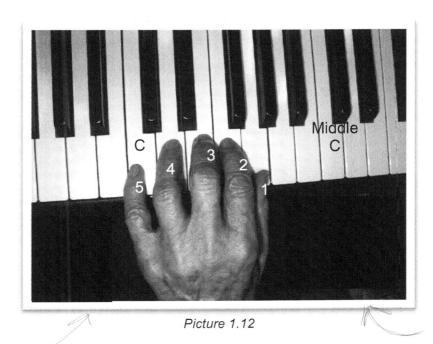

Picture 1.12

The fifth finger plays the white key to the left of the group of 2 black keys.

After you have played fingers **5 4 3 2 1**, the **next key up is played with the third finger**.

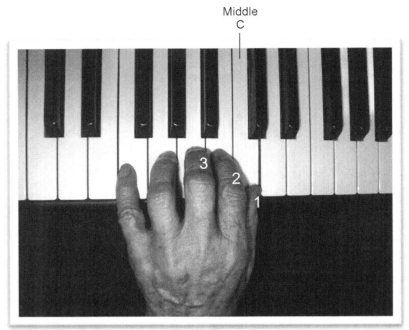

Picture 1.13

Swing your third finger over your thumb and play the next key up to the right.

Play fingers: **2, 1**, reaching Middle C.

Proceed back down the scale again, playing fingers: **2, 3**.

After you have played the third finger, tuck your thumb under the third to play the next white key down (to the left).

Play fingers **1 2 3 4 5**, ending on C.

You have just played the C Major scale with your left hand!

(ii) Now play the same scale again, **singing what you play**.

Continue playing and singing this scale three or more times until you have its sound firmly fixed in your ear and brain.

(iii) **Now try singing the scale without playing it.** Don't forget to check yourself.

Congratulations! You are well on your way to having a "good ear!"

PLAY BY EAR IN THE KEY OF C MAJOR - INSTANTLY

Don't think you're ready for this yet? We know you are!

All songs in the key of C major are made up of notes from the C scale – the seven white keys on the keyboard: **C D E F G A B**

We know what you're thinking – "Only seven keys? This IS easy!" You're right!

And with the first song you're going to play by ear, you'll see it's even easier than that, because there are **only 5 keys in the whole song**!

Exercise #25

(i) Remember the melody you played in **Exercise #18** on page 16?
In the right hand C five-finger position, you played finger numbers: **3 2 1 2 3 3 3**

Did you notice that you were playing the first seven notes of "Mary had a Little Lamb"?

(ii) Play the phrase again, singing "Mary had a little lamb"

(iii) Now continue singing the song – the next line is "little lamb".
Repeat that phrase and see if you can match the piano key to your voice. You'll notice the three syllables are all on the same note.

(YES! IT'S THE NEXT NOTE TO THE LEFT – AND YOU CAN PLAY IT WITH FINGER NUMBER 2 IF YOU WANT)

(iv) Sing the next "little lamb" and try to find the notes on the keyboard. You'll notice the melody skips a note here. Remember, there are only 5 notes and all the notes are under your five fingers.

(YES! "LITTLE LAMB" IS UNDER FINGER NUMBERS 3 AND 5)

(v) Sing the next phrase: "Mary had a little lamb".
Find the notes on the keyboard. Easy – it's the same as the beginning.

(vi) Now sing the last phrase: "Its fleece was white as snow".
Repeat singing this phrase. Don't play anything until you have made careful note of when the notes go up and when they go down.
When you feel you know the direction of the melody, find the notes on the keyboard.

Congratulations! You have just played a song by ear!

PRACTICE MAKES PERFECT

Don't stop here! Play and sing "Mary Had a Little Lamb" several times until you don't make any mistakes.

PLAYING MORE SONGS BY EAR

Songs are in many different keys, but the good thing is that, **even if a song is written in one key, when you play by ear, you can play it in any key** you choose.

We like the key of C for beginners. Before you're ready to play more songs by ear, you should know some facts that will help you play by ear.

CLUES THAT A SONG IS IN THE KEY OF C MAJOR

How do we know a song is in the key of C MAJOR? If you have musical training this is easy. For those with no training, there are three clues to help you.

1) Songs in the key of C major usually have **only white notes** in the melody.

2) Songs in the key of C major usually **end on a C note**.

3) Songs in the key of C major usually **end with a C chord**.

Test this theory on "Mary Had a Little Lamb". See if these clues tell you that it is written in the key of C Major.

1) Are all the notes in the song played on white keys?

2) Does the song end on a C note?

3) Does the C chord sound right on the last note of "Mary's Lamb"?

> **Try it:** You've played a C chord before in exercises #22 and #23. In the C five-finger position play fingers 1, 3, 5 together to sound a C Major chord.
>
> Play **the C note with your right hand and the C chord with your left hand**. Sound right? Good – because it is.

By answering yes to the 3 clue questions above, we can deduce that we played "Mary Had a Little Lamb" in the key of C major.

Let's see how the clues can help you play other songs by ear in the key of C major.

HOW DO YOU START TO PLAY A SONG BY EAR?

You have to find the first note of the song, right? Unfortunately for "ear-players", **songs don't always start on the first note of the scale**.
For example, "Mary Had a Little Lamb" starts on the third note of the C major scale, E.

Exercise #26: Play "Jingle Bells" by Ear

When you sing a song without the musical backing, it could be in any key.
We want to make sure that you sing your first songs in the key of C major.

So, to do this we **use the clues**:

1) "Jingle Bells" is going to be played on **only white notes**.
2) The **last note is C**.
3) The **last chord is a C major chord**.

To find the first note, we will start with the last note and chord, which we know are both C!

Follow these steps:

(i) Sing "Jingle Bells" sitting in front of the keyboard.

When you get to the last word, "sleigh", play the C note.

Adjust your singing until you sing the C note on "sleigh".

(ii) Sing "One horse open sleigh" several times until you land on the C note without a mistake.

(iii) Sing it again softly playing the C chord (left hand) and C note (right hand) on "sleigh".

Now sing the first word: "Jingle" and find that first note on the keyboard.

Clues: It is a higher note than the C you sang on "sleigh".
It is one of the notes of the C chord.

Keep singing "Jingle" until you find the correct note on the keyboard.

(iv) Once you find the first note, sing the song starting on that note and **play the notes you sing.** There are quite a few skips and jumps in this song, so be careful.

The good thing is there are **only five notes in the tune**! C D E F and G.

If you **keep your hand in the C five finger position**, you will have all the notes you need for the song under those five fingers.

Exercise #27: More Songs to Play in the Key of C Major

The following songs have only 5 notes and can be played in the key of C major with your right hand in the C five-finger position.

Go ahead and try them. Remember to use the clues to help you. Good Luck!

"Beautiful Brown Eyes"
"When the Saints Go Marching In"
"Ode to Joy"

ADDING A LEFT HAND ACCOMPANIMENT - INSTANTLY

This is a bonus for those students who want to take the challenge a step further.
If you don't want to do this section, you can move on to the next section and return to this at any time you want.

Some people feel that you're not REALLY playing the piano until you play it with BOTH HANDS. It is true that when you play with both hands, you potentially have a whole orchestra under your fingers. You can give the rhythm, harmony and the bass support to a melody, making it much livelier than just picking out single melody notes with one hand.

Playing with both hands isn't easy and, like everything, requires practice to get really good at it. For those who are ready for the challenge, here's an Instant, quick and easy way to add a left hand accompaniment to your songs.

We can begin with your first song: "Mary Had a Little Lamb". Once you have practiced your song so that you can play the right hand with no mistakes, you are ready to add the left hand.

Exercise #28: Adding a Bass Note

The bass in a band or orchestra gives a solid foundation to the harmony and beat of a song. You can do the same for your song by playing **one note in the left hand**. In this exercise you have the option of learning the names of some of the notes. You can still do the exercise without knowing the names. At this stage, we leave it up to you.

(i) **Put both hands on the keyboard as shown in Picture 1.14.**
Each finger should have one note under it.

This is the "**C five-finger position**".

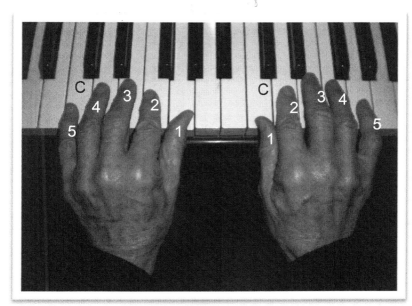
Picture 1.14

Notice that **both hands are over the same note names** an octave apart.

The names of the notes are written on the keyboard.

They are the **notes of the alphabet: C D E F G**

The fingers of both hands are numbered.

Notice that in the **right hand, finger number 1 is on the C note**, but in the **left hand it is finger number 5 that is on C.**

(ii) **Play the RIGHT HAND** starting with finger number 1, going upwards to 5.

Sing the finger numbers: 1 2 3 4 5 as you play the notes upwards.

Then **play the notes downwards** and sing finger numbers: 5 4 3 2 1

(iii) If you want to learn the names of the notes you can:

Play the same notes, but now **sing the letter names** upwards: C D E F G

Then go **downwards** and sing: G F E D C

(iv) **Play the LEFT HAND** starting with finger number 5, going upwards to 1.

Sing the finger numbers: 5 4 3 2 1 as you play the notes upwards.

Then **play the notes downwards** and sing the finger numbers: 1 2 3 4 5

(v) If you want to learn the names of the notes you can:

Play the same notes, but now **sing the letter names** upwards: C D E F G

Then go **downwards** and sing: G F E D C

"MARY HAD A LITTLE LAMB" WITH A BASS NOTE IN THE LEFT HAND:

Keep your right and left hands in the same positions as the previous exercise – the C five-finger position.

Below are the lyrics to "Mary Had a Little Lamb" with the finger numbers of both the right and left hands. This may look complicated at first, because it has many elements to it.

There's a simple explanation:

The **lyrics** are the words of the song. Since there is no written music, we use the lyrics as a guide.

Notice that some of the words are broken up by hyphens into syllables so that there is one syllable for each note played.

The letters (C and G) above the lyrics are the **chord symbols**. You'll learn more about them later.

The vertical lines are **bar-lines** dividing the beats into bars. More about that later.

Above the lyrics are the **finger numbers of the RIGHT hand**.

With your hands in the **C five-finger position**, the notes under the finger numbers are the **same notes you played by ear.** You already know the tune so you can ignore those finger numbers or use them as a guide.

The LEFT hand finger numbers show you when to play the bass notes.
Note that there are only two bass notes and they are played on the first beat in each bar.

Let's try the song, remembering to play slowly and carefully.

> ***TIP:*** *Only move on to step (ii) and (iii) of this exercise when you have completed the previous step without mistakes.*

(i) Play the **right hand only**. You may sing along if you can.

(ii) **Sing the lyrics** and **play only the left hand notes** on the correct beats.

(iii) **Play both hands together**. Play slowly and carefully.

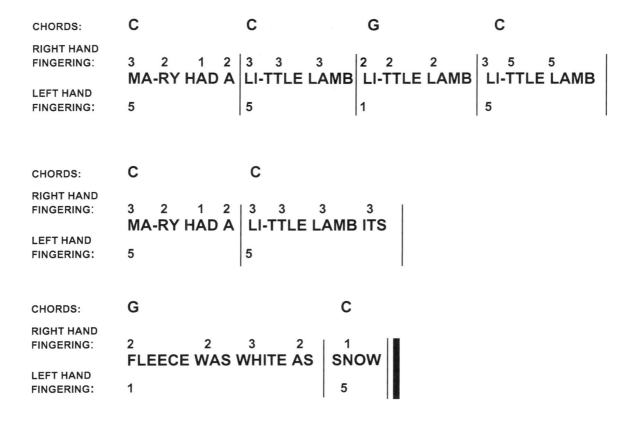

Exercise #29: Adding Chords in the Left Hand

In the five-finger position, when you play fingers 1, 3 and 5 simultaneously, you are playing a chord. **Try it:**

(i) **In the C five-finger position, play the notes under fingers 1, 3 and 5 all at the same time.** You can play the left and right hand separately, or you can play them together.

   You have just played a C major chord.

   The chord symbols above the lyrics tell you that the **other chord in the song is the G major chord.**

(ii) **Find the G note.** It's the fifth note of the C five-finger position (C D E F G).

(iii) **Start a new five-finger position with G as the lowest note.** In your **right hand**, finger number 1 will be on G and in your **left hand**, finger number 5 will be on G. **You are now in the G five-finger position.**

   Picture 1.15 below shows both hands in the G five-finger position.

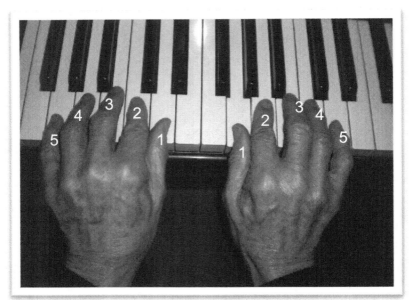

Picture 1.15

(iv) **Play the RIGHT HAND** starting with finger number 1, going upwards to 5
Sing the finger numbers: 1 2 3 4 5 as you play the notes upwards.
Then **play the notes downwards** and sing finger numbers: 5 4 3 2 1

(v) If you want to learn the names of the notes you can:
Play the same notes, but now **sing the letter names** upwards: G A B C D
Then go **downwards** and sing: D C B A G

(vi) **Play the LEFT HAND** starting with finger number 5, going upwards to 1
Sing the finger numbers: 5 4 3 2 1 as you play the notes upwards.
Then **play the notes downwards** and sing the finger numbers: 1 2 3 4 5

(vii) If you want to learn the names of the notes you can:
Play the same notes, but now **sing the letter names** upwards: G A B C D
Then go **downwards** and sing: D C B A G

(viii) Now play the G chord with your right hand. First play the notes under fingers **1 3 5** separately, then play them simultaneously.

(ix) Now play the G chord with your left hand. First play the notes under fingers **5 3 1** separately, then play them simultaneously.

You have just played a G major chord!

(x) **Practice playing a C major chord to a G major chord.** You can practice playing each hand separately or playing the chords in both hands until you feel confident that you can get from one chord to the next without making a mistake.

PLAY "MARY HAD A LITTLE LAMB" ADDING MAJOR CHORDS IN THE LEFT HAND:

To start, have **your right and left hands in the C five-finger position.**

The right hand stays in the same C position throughout the song.

Remember that **your left hand is going to change to the G five-finger position during the song -** on the second "little" and then on "fleece"

Your **left hand follows the chord symbols** above the lyrics.

When there's a C major chord symbol, you play the **C major chord** and when there's a G major chord symbol, you play a **G major chord.**

(i) **Sing the lyrics** and play the chords with the left hand only.

C	C	G	C
MA-RY HAD A	LI-TTLE LAMB	LI-TTLE LAMB	LI-TTLE LAMB

C	C	G	C
MA-RY HAD A	LI-TTLE LAMB ITS	FLEECE WAS WHITE AS	SNOW

(ii) Once you feel confident try playing the tune with the right hand.
You will be playing both hands together.

Exercise #30: Two Hand Accompaniment

Sometimes you may just want to sing the song and play along, giving your voice some backing. Here's an easy way you can do that:

Sing the lyrics.

Play the bass notes with your left hand on the first beat of each bar.

Play the chords with your right hand in the middle of each bar.

The order of your hands playing goes: LEFT RIGHT LEFT RIGHT and so on.

Remember that the **left hand stays in the C five-finger position** and the **right hand starts in the C five-finger position and changes to the G five-finger position** to play the G major chord.

Notice that the **names of the bass notes** your left hand plays **are the same as the names of the chord symbols.** Finger 5 plays a C and finger 1 plays a G.
This is because the bass notes are actually the bass or root notes of the chord.

When you see a chord symbol, instead of playing a chord in the left hand, you can always play just a single note with that same letter name. More about this later.

BONUS EXERCISE: PLAYING MAJOR CHORDS IN BOTH HANDS

For variety, you can replace the single bass note with a chord in the left hand. The left hand plays a chord at the beginning of the bar and the right hand plays the chord in the middle of the bar.

There are many more fun and easy ways you can accompany your singing.
You'll learn more as you progress through the book.

Exercise #31: Play "Jingle Bells" with Both Hands

Play "Jingle Bells" by ear. Play the bass notes or play the chords with both hands.

C	C	C	C
JIN - GLE BELLS	JIN - GLE BELLS	JIN - GLE ALL THE	WAY

F	C	G	G
OH WHAT FUN IT	IS TO RIDE A	ONE HORSE O – PEN	SLEIGH HEY

C	C	C	C
JIN - GLE BELLS	JIN - GLE BELLS	JIN - GLE ALL THE	WAY

F	C	G	C
OH WHAT FUN IT	IS TO RIDE A	ONE HORSE O – PEN	SLEIGH

Exercise #32: The F Major Chord

The chord symbols tell you there's a new chord in this song – the F major chord. Can you play it?

Clue: *You play a C major chord starting in the C five-finger position and a G major chord starting in the G five-finger position. The same will be true with the F chord.*

(i)   Put the first finger of your right hand on the F note.
      (Count up from Middle C D E F)

(ii) Put your hand into the five-finger position starting on F.

(iii) Play the notes under finger numbers 1, 3 and 5 simultaneously.
      This is an F major chord. The notes of the F major chord are F A C.

(iv) Put finger number 5 of your left hand on the F below middle C. Get into the F five-finger position and play an F major chord – under fingers 5, 3 and 1.

(v)   Practice playing both hands together, alternating one hand at a time and even the F bass note in the left hand followed by the F chord in the right hand.
      Be creative – have fun

(vi) Once you feel confident in playing F chord, practice going from the C chord to the F chord and back. And also going from C chord to G major chord and back to C chord again. Do this with separate hands and together and all the combinations you tried in (v).

If you don't want to play the melody, you can have fun singing and playing "Jingle Bells" by just playing the accompaniments.

Try:

(i)   keeping the beat by playing major chords in both hands on every beat or

(ii) alternating hands, with the left hand playing the bass notes (or chords) on the first beat of the bar and the right hand playing the chords in the middle of the bar.

Here's a guide to help you out:

```
        C              |        C              |        C              |        C
3   3   3              | 3   3  3              | 3   5  1   2   3      |
JIN-GLE BELLS          | JIN-GLE BELLS         | JIN-GLE ALL THE WAY   |
5                      | 5                     | 5                     | 5

        F              |        C              |        G              |        G
4   4   4   4          | 4  3   3   3          | 3   2  2   3   2      | 5
OH WHAT FUN IT         | IS TO RIDE A          | ONE HORSE O – PEN SLEIGH | HEY
2                      | 5                     | 1                     | 1

        C              |        C              |        C              |        C
JIN-GLE BELLS          | JIN-GLE BELLS         | JIN-GLE ALL THE WAY   |
5                      | 5                     | 5                     | 5

        F              |        C              |        G              |        C
                       |                       | 5   5  4   2   1      |
OH WHAT FUN IT         | IS TO RIDE A          | ONE HORSE O – PEN SLEIGH |
2                      | 5                     | 1              5      |
```

Exercise #33: "Play Beautiful Brown Eyes" With Both Hands

Play the accompaniment for "Beautiful Brown Eyes" by reading the chord symbols (C F G) above the lyrics. You can choose to play either bass notes or chords in the left hand.

C	C	F	F
BEAU- TI – FUL	BEAU- TI – FUL	BROWN EYES	

C	C	G	G
BEAU- TI – FUL	BEAU- TI – FUL	BROWN	EYES

C	C	F	F
BEAU- TI – FUL	BEAU- TI – FUL	BROWN EYES	I'LL

G	G	C	C
NE-VER LOVE	BLUE EYES A -	GAIN	

Exercise #34: Accompaniment in Waltz Time

"Beautiful Brown Eyes" is written in **WALTZ TIME**, meaning that there are only **3 beats in a bar.** If you go back to page 39 you will notice that "Jingle Bells" has 4 beats in a bar.

Instead of:
BEAU - TI – FUL | BEAU - TI – FUL | BROWN   EYES |

Sing:
One - two – three | One - two – three | One - two – three | One - two –three |

Because it is a **waltz**, when you sing this song and play the accompaniment, alternating between left and right hands, you **play the left hand chord or bass note on the first beat of the bar,** but you will want to **play the chords twice in the right hand**.

Like this:

C C	C C	F F	F F
BEAU- TI – FUL	BEAU- TI – FUL	BROWN EYES	
5	5	2	2

Practice playing the whole song in this way.

Exercise #35: "When the Saints Go Marching In"

This song is played using the **C five-finger position** (Picture 1.14)
Once you have picked out the melody by ear, try the accompaniment for this song.
We have written the chord symbols to help you out. Remember that you can play either bass notes or chords in the left hand.

Notice that the first chord symbol, C, starts before the lyrics.
That's because the melody only begins after the first beat of the bar.

You'll also notice lots of gaps in the lyrics. But remember that the silences (or holds) have a time value too. We have marked them with (*) to remind you. This is the start of learning rhythmic and note values. We will talk more about that later.

```
C                   | C              | C                 | C           |
* OH WHEN THE       | SAINTS * * *   | * GO MARCH – ING  | IN * * *    |

C                   | C              | C                 | G           |
* OH WHEN THE       | SAINTS * GO *  | MARCH *- ING  *   | IN * * *    |

G                   | C              | C                 | F           |
* I WANT TO         | BE   * * *     | IN  *    THAT *   | NUM * – BER |

F                   | C              | C         G       | C           ||
*  * WHEN THE       | SAINTS * GO *  | MARCH *– ING  *   | IN          
```

WHAT TO DO NEXT?

If you've enjoyed playing by ear, you can continue with that.
Look ahead at the song titles in this book and see how many you can play by ear.
They're all in the key of C major with the same chords – C, F and G.

Or, you can move on to the next section and learn
HOW TO READ MUSIC - INSTANTLY.

CHAPTER 2: GETTING ACQUAINTED WITH THE KEYBOARD

THE KEYBOARD PATTERN

When you look at a keyboard don't be intimidated by the seemingly disorganized jumble of black and white keys confronting you. You will learn that the keyboard is actually organized brilliantly, making it so much simpler than it looks at first glance.

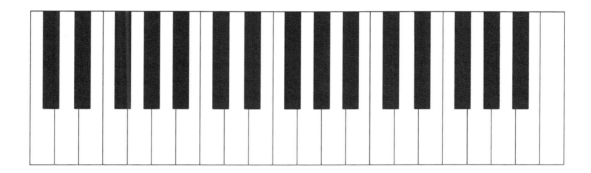

Notice that the black and white keys alternate much of the time, going: white, black, white, black, except where there are two white keys placed together.

When these two consecutive white keys appear, they force **the black keys into two specific groupings**: a group of **two black keys** and a group of **three black keys**.

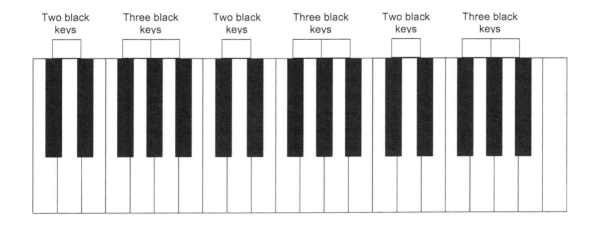

Exercise #36

The layout of the keyboard is one of the reasons why it is a wonderful instrument to play on. You will learn that you don't have to look at your hands at all and you can find notes easily through feeling you way around the pattern of black and white keys.

Close your eyes and feel for the black keys. Start at the bottom of the keyboard and feel your way up, noting when you are on a group of two or a group of three black keys.

Take special note of the pair of white keys that separate the groups of black keys.

From this exercise you can see that, because of the grouping of the raised black keys, it is **easy to tell exactly where you are on the keyboard**.

You are beginning to see the **importance of "position" in music**.
This will become clearer as you progress in your musical education.

BLACK AND WHITE KEYS

The pattern of the black keys helps us find the white keys.

Here's how: Find the group of two black keys in the **middle** of the keyboard.
Play them with your index and middle fingers (finger numbers 2 and 3) of your right hand.

You will notice that your thumb (first finger) is over the white key to the immediate left of the group of two black keys. Play that white key.

This white key is called **"Middle C"**, because it is the C key in the middle of the piano.

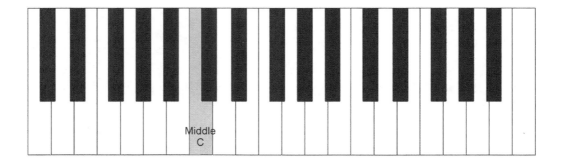

The pattern of the keys is repeated over and over on the keyboard.

When you play a note in a particular position on the keyboard, every other note in the same position has the same name and the same sound, only at a higher or lower pitch.

FINDING "A"

The musical alphabet has seven letters: A B C D E F G

Just as we have written the alphabet from left to right, the keys on the keyboard are named from left to right in ascending order. So, when you are on C and you want to find the A key, you go two white keys to the left.

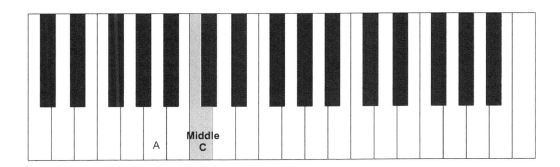

THE NAMES OF THE WHITE KEYS

Starting on **A**, each white key going upwards to the right on the keyboard, takes the next letter of the alphabet. So, after **A** are **B C D E F G**

Notice in the diagram below that once you have named the keys with the seven letters, **A B C D E F G**, the next key up is **A** once again.

The letter names are always in the same positions relative to the black keys.
The pattern is repeated throughout the keyboard.

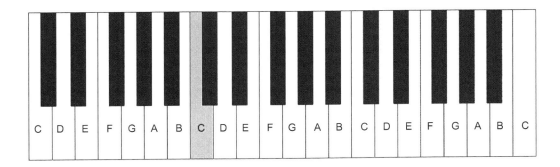

OCTAVES

There are seven letters in the musical alphabet and they are repeated as you go upwards on the keyboard. The eighth letter is the same as the first letter.

If you start with any of the letters, and count eight keys up or down, you will land on the same letter name.

This **space between notes of the same name is called an Octave**. So, for example, if you start on Middle C and play the next C up, you will be playing C an **octave higher**. The next C down from Middle C is an **octave lower**.

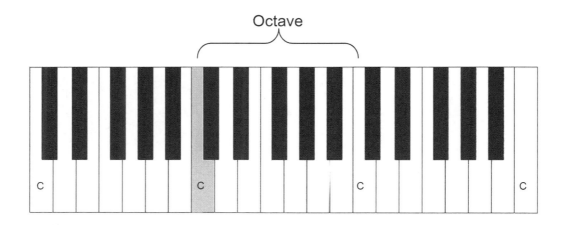

You should be able to play notes an octave apart in one hand.

Try it with your right hand: Put your first finger (thumb) on Middle C and play the next C up with your fifth finger.

Try the same with your left hand, playing Middle C and the lower C with your first and fifth fingers.

FINDING NOTES ON THE KEYBOARD

When you want to find a particular letter name on the keyboard, you can always start by finding **Middle C** and then spelling the alphabet upwards or downwards to find the letter name you want.

The best way to gain confidence about the names of the white keys is to **memorize their position relative to the black keys**. Below are some diagrams and exercises to help.

Using the Group of Two Black Keys as Markers:

You already know where **C** is

Play all the C's you can find on the keyboard.

D is in the middle of the group of two black keys.

Play all the D's you can find on the keyboard.

C and E are positioned on either side of the group of black keys.

Play all the E's you can find on the keyboard.

Exercise #37

Once you have memorized the positions of C, D and E, test yourself by playing those three keys in random order, saying or singing aloud their names.

Now find the following keys from memory: **D C E C | E D E C | D E C E | D C E C**

 Note: To make this Exercise more challenging, jump around on the keyboard so that you are not using the same group of two black keys to find all the notes. For example, play the first D low down, the next C high up, and then Find the E in the Middle of the Keyboard.

On the *outside* of the group of three black keys are the notes **F** (on the left) and **B** (on the right)

Play all the F's you can find on the keyboard.

Play all the B's you can find on the keyboard.

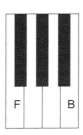

On the *inside* of the group of three black keys are **G** (on the left) and **A** (on the right)

Play all the G's you can find on the keyboard.

Play all the A's you can find on the keyboard.

Exercise #38

Take the time to memorize the position of the notes (F, G, A, B) on the Keyboard. Once you have done so, test yourself by playing and singing those four keys (F, G, A, B) in random order.

Now **play the following notes**, finding them from memory and not by counting from the preceding note:

G B F A | G A F B | A F B G | B F A B | F B A G

Make the test more challenging by jumping around on the keyboard so that you are not using the same big group of three black keys to find the notes.

CHAPTER 3: BASICS OF WRITTEN MUSIC

Since this book is an "Instant" method, you only have to learn the
music theory absolutely necessary to get you playing the keyboard.
The information below outlines the basics of reading musical notation.

MUSICAL LAYOUT

If you look at most Keyboard sheet music, you will notice that there are two symbols at the beginning of the **GRAND STAFF**, a **TREBLE CLEF** and a **BASS CLEF**.

> ***Note:*** *The Treble Clef is also known as the G Clef.*
> *The Bass Clef is also known as the F Clef.*

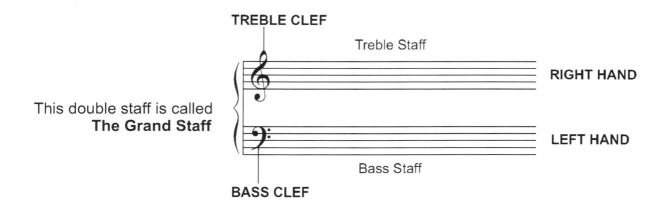

Music notes are written on the lines and spaces of the staff.
Each has a specific letter name of the musical alphabet - A B C D E F G

Notes placed on the staff indicate exactly where on the keyboard the note is to be played.

Notes placed on the **Treble staff** are **high notes** played on the right side of the keyboard, and are usually played with the **right hand**.

Notes written on the **Bass staff** are low notes and are played on the left side of the keyboard with the **left hand**.

Below is a **diagram showing how written music corresponds to the keys on the keyboard**.

Notice that there are many more keys on the keyboard than there are lines and spaces on the staff.

When you get past the last line and space on the staff, **ledger lines** are added to indicate notes that are higher or lower than the staff. Middle C is on a ledger line between the treble and bass staves.

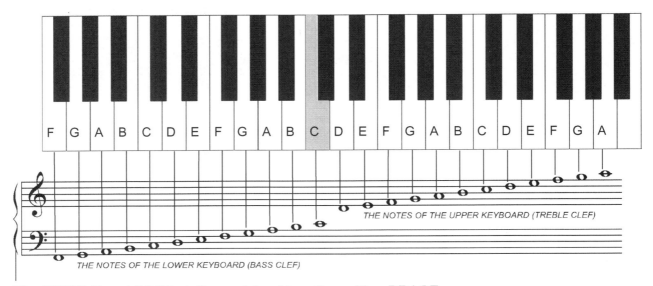

The TREBLE and BASS staffs are joined together with a BRACE.

This diagram may look confusing because it has so many notes and labels.
But don't worry; we don't expect you to memorize it.

In the INSTANT method, we read only the notes in the treble staff for the right hand and the chord symbols for the left hand.

MUSICAL NOTES

A music note placed on the staff tells you its pitch (high or low) and the shape of the note tells you its duration (how long to hold it). You will learn about the shapes and time values of notes later.

Notice in the diagram below that Middle C is positioned below the Treble Staff on its own ledger line.

Starting at Middle C and going upwards, the letters, in alphabetical order, go from the Middle C line up to the next space (D), to the next line (E), and so on.
When the G line is reached, the next space up is A.

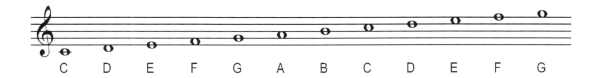

The same way you learned the names of the keys through their positioning on the keyboard, you should learn the names of the musical notes through their position on the staff.

The **FIVE LINES** of the **Treble Staff** are **E G B D F**

Here's a sentence to help you remember the note names of the Treble clef lines:

Every **G**ood **B**oy **D**eserves **F**un

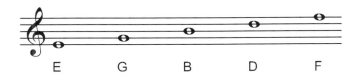

The **FOUR SPACES** on the **Treble staff** are **F A C E**

To learn the space notes on the Treble Staff just remember the word **"FACE"**.

Finding Notes on the Keyboard

For this exercise you have to combine your knowledge of the positions of keys on the keyboard, with your new knowledge of the names of the lines and spaces of the Treble Staff.

Test yourself by playing and singing the notes on the staff below.

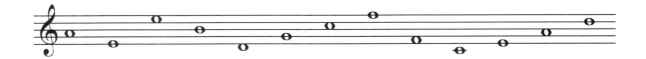

HAND POSITIONS

You can use any fingers to play a song on the keyboard, but you will find it much easier in the long run if you get accustomed to the correct hand positions early.

By using the correct hand positions you won't have to look down for notes, instead you will be able to feel your way around the keyboard as professional musicians do.

C POSITION - RIGHT HAND

Place your first finger on Middle C.
Your other four fingers should naturally rest on the keys D E F G.

The C five-finger position is pictured in the diagram below.

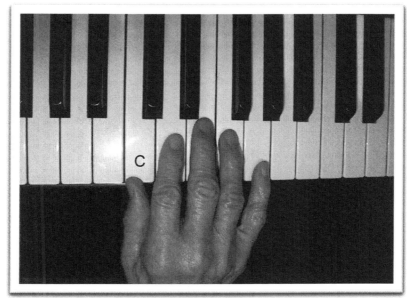

Picture 3.1

Play the keys under your fingers slowly and firmly, releasing each key after you play it so that the sounds do not blend together.

Picture 3.2 shows the five notes of the C five-finger position written on the Treble Staff.

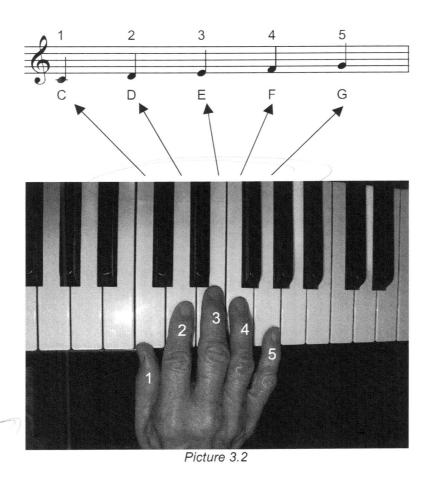

Picture 3.2

DIRECTIONAL READING - SKIPS AND STEPS

Once you know the names of the notes on the keyboard and on the staff, you are ready to combine that knowledge with **"directional reading"**.
This means that instead of playing songs by finding one note at a time, we also notice **the direction** the notes move on the staff, and **how far** they move.

When notes move **upwards** on the staff, they sound higher, and are played towards the **right** of the keyboard. Play these notes:

If a melody goes from a **line** up to the very **next space**, or from a space to the next line, it is moving **up one step**, so play the **next key** to the right.
Play these notes:

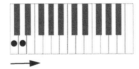  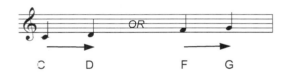

If a melody goes from a **line** up to the **next line**, skipping the space, then you move to the right on the keyboard, skipping a note. Or if a melody goes from a **space** up to the **next space**, skipping a line, then you move to the right, skipping a note.
Play these notes:

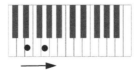 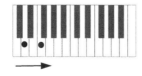 

When notes move **downwards** on the staff, they sound lower, and are played more towards the **left** on the keyboard.
Play these notes:

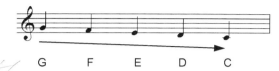 

When a melody goes from a **space** down to **the very next line**, or from a line to the next space, it is moving down **one step**, so play the **next key** to the left on the keyboard.
Play these notes:

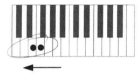  

If a melody goes from a **line** down to the **next line**, skipping a space, then you move to the left on the keyboard, skipping out a note. Or when a melody goes down from a **space to the next space**, skipping out a line, then you also skip out a note on the keyboard.
Play these notes:

  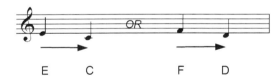

Once you get used to directional reading, playing becomes easier because you don't have to think of the name of every note as you play – you simply start at the first note and follow the melody's direction of steps, skips or jumps.

SONGS IN THE C FIVE-FINGER POSITION

We chose well-known melodies for you to begin with since you have not yet learned about timing in music. At this stage you should play the timing from memory.

All of these melodies are made up of only five notes – C D E F G

They are the notes **under your fingers** in the **C five-finger position**.

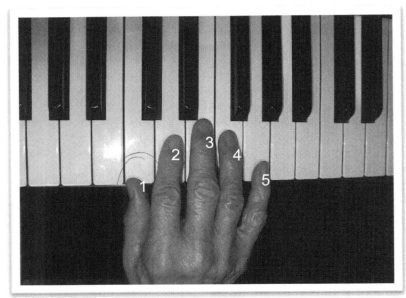

Picture 3.3

"ODE TO JOY"

These melody notes move in **steps**. For the correct finger positions follow the numbers above the notes. The "hold" reminds you to hold those notes longer.

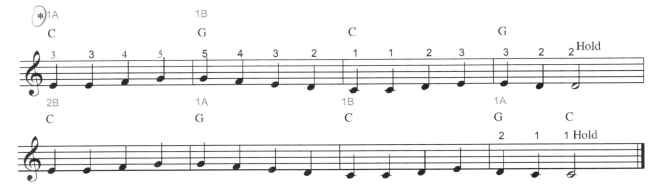

(*)The grey numbers and letters above the chord symbols are suggested accompaniment patterns. You will learn more about this later (p. 122)

"MERRILY WE ROLL ALONG"

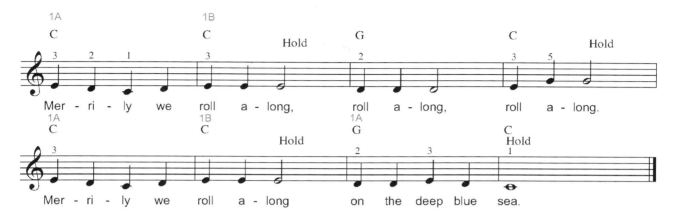

"LIGHTLY ROW"

This melody moves in steps and skips.

"ODE TO JOY" – THE FULL THEME

This version of "Ode to Joy" has a melody that moves in steps, skips and jumps.
A JUMP leaves out **more than one note** as it moves to the next melody note.

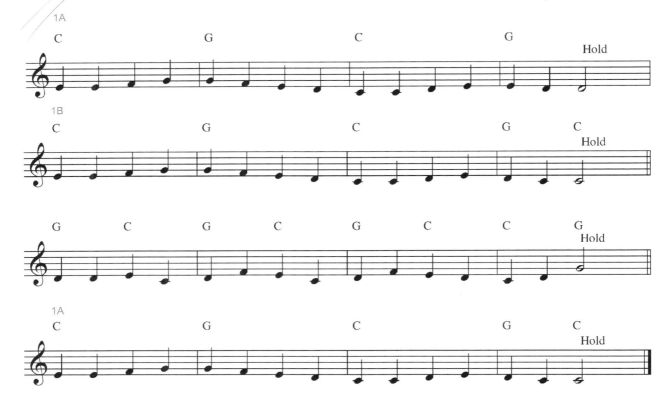

Practice these melodies until you can play them with confidence.
Once you've achieved that, you are ready to add the left hand.

ADDING THE LEFT HAND

Some people feel that you're not really playing the piano until you play with both hands.
It is true that when you play with both hands, you potentially have a whole orchestra under your fingers. You can give rhythm, harmony and bass support to a melody.

Playing with both hands isn't easy and requires practice to become proficient.
For those who are ready for the challenge, here's the "Instant" way to add a left hand accompaniment to your songs.

C FIVE-FINGER POSITION WITH THE LEFT HAND

Place your left hand in the C five-finger position with your fifth finger on the C an octave below Middle C

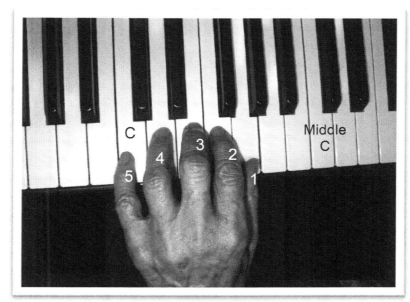

Picture 3.4

To exercise your fingers, practice playing the notes one by one, starting with your fifth finger, going up to the first finger and then down again.

Say or sing the letter names as you play: **C D E F G**. Do this exercise several times until it feels natural.

Now play the following notes with fingers 5 and 1: **C G G C C C G G C**
                                                                        5 1 1 5 5 5 1 1 5

You're now ready to add a bass line to your song.

ADDING A BASS NOTE

The bass in a band or orchestra adds a steady beat to a song.
You can do the same for your songs by simply **playing one note in the left hand**.

Put **both hands in the C five-finger position** and play "Ode to Joy", "Merrily We Roll Along" and "Lightly Row" again but **this time:**

    (i)   Play the notes on the staff with the right hand.
    (ii)   Play the notes Indicated by the letters above the staff (C and G) at the same time the right hand melody is sounded
    (iii)   Hold the bass note down until a new bass note is indicated.

CHAPTER 4: PLAYING CHORDS

Once you've got the hang of playing the bass notes,
it's an easy step to play chords in the left hand.

The letters C and G above the staff that you followed to play the bass notes
are actually **chord symbols**. Up to now you have played only the bass note of the chord,
but, once you've got the hang of adding the left hand, you're ready to play the whole chord.

INSTANT CHORDS

In the five-finger position, **when you play fingers 1 3 and 5 simultaneously, you are playing a chord**. Try it:

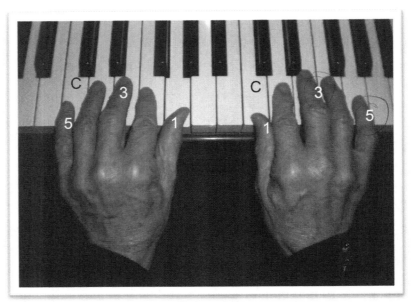

Picture 4.1

(i) **In the C five-finger position, play C E G separately.**
The notes are under fingers 1, 3 and 5 in the right hand.
In the left hand the notes C E G are under fingers 5, 3 and 1.

(ii) **Now play those notes all at the same time.**
You have just played a C major chord.
The notes of the **C major chord** are **C E G**

(iii) Practice playing **a melody and chords** by playing the **chord in the left hand and separate notes C E G (broken chord) in the right hand.**

You can be creative and play the C, E and G notes in any order, making a melody.
For example you can play: **C E G, G E C, E G C, C G E, G C E, C E G**

(iv)   Now switch hands and play the chord in the right hand and broken chord in the left hand..

You will see that the **other chord symbol in the songs is the G major chord.**

Here's how you find the G major chord:

(i)   **Find the G note.** It's the fifth note of the C five-finger position (C D E F G).

(ii)   **Start a new five-finger position with G as the lowest note.**

   In your **right hand,** finger number 1 will be on G
   In your **left hand** finger number 5 will be on G.
   You are now in the G five-finger position.

The diagram shows **both hands in the G five-finger position playing a G major chord**.

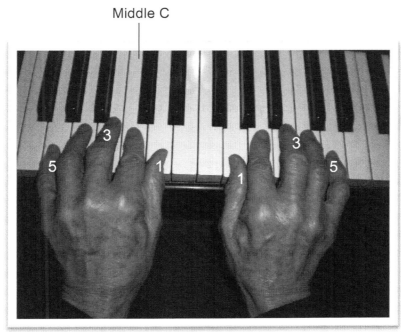

Picture 4.2

(iii)   In the G position play the notes under fingers 1, 3, and 5.
   The notes are **G B D**. You have just played a G major chord.
   Practice playing a G major chord with both hands.

(iv)   Play chords and broken chords in both hands as you did with exercise numbers (iii) and (iv) for the C chord.

(v)   **Practice going from a C major chord to a G major chord.**
   You can practice playing each hand separately or playing the chords in both hands until you feel confident that you can get smoothly from one chord to the next.

MELODIES WITH CHORDS IN THE LEFT HAND

Play "Ode to Joy", "Merrily We Roll Along" and "Lightly Row" again, playing chords in the left hand when you see the chord symbols above the staff.

(i) **Play the left hand only. Sing the melody or the lyrics** and play the chords with the left hand. Practice this until you feel confident.

(ii) Now play the melody with your right hand and chords with your left hand.

To start, **your right and left hands are in the C five-finger position. The right hand stays in the C five-finger position for the whole song.**

But remember that **your left hand is going to change to the G five-finger position during the song** as directed by the chord symbols.

THE F MAJOR CHORD

Following the Instant method, you already know that a chord is formed by playing **notes 1 3 and 5 in a five-finger position**.

See if you can **play an F major chord in both hands**.
Look at the guide below only after you have tried it alone.

(i) Find F on the keyboard

(ii) Start a five-finger position on F. Your fingers will be over F G A B C

(iii) Play the notes with both hands, saying the letter-names.

(iv) Play F A C notes with fingers 1 3 5 in both hands.

(v) Now play the F major chord with the left and right hands separately and together.

(vi) Play chords and broken chords in both hands as you did with the previous exercises.

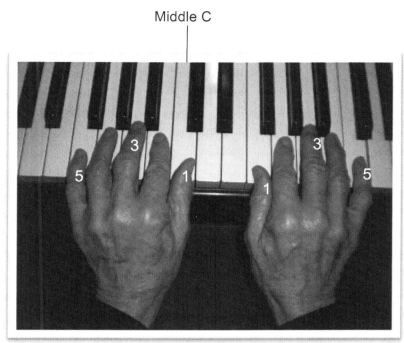

Picture 4.3

Practice the chords, going from C major to F major to G major and back to the C major chord, until you feel confident that you can find each position easily.

bold   C   F   G
~~CMaj~~   ~~FMaj~~   ~~GMaj~~

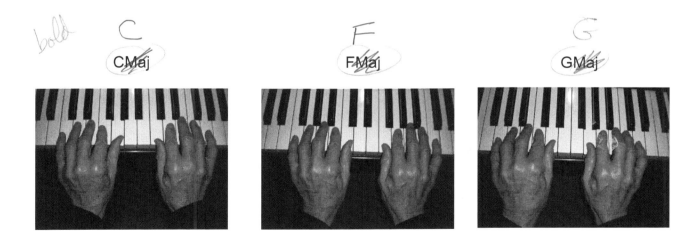

Believe it or not, you have just played a chord combination (C F G) that you could easily use to accompany any song in the key of C major!

MELODIES IN FIVE-FINGER POSITIONS

Now that you have been introduced to reading melodies with steps, skips and jumps as well as playing bass notes and chords from chord symbols, you should sharpen your skills and get more experience playing some new songs.

The melodies of "Jingle Bells" and "When the Saints Go Marching In" are under just five-fingers and the chords are C, F and G major.

"JINGLE BELLS"

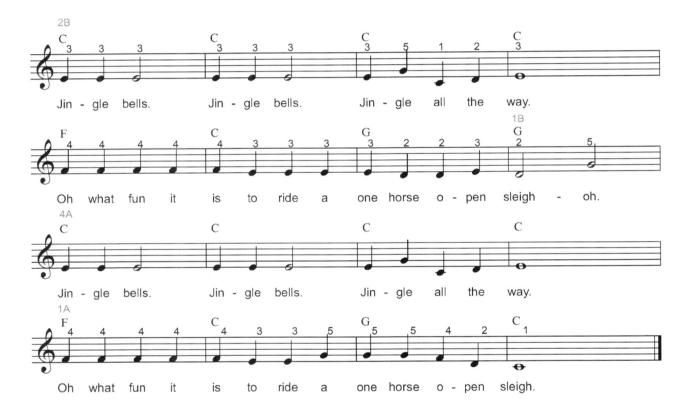

"WHEN THE SAINTS GO MARCHING IN"

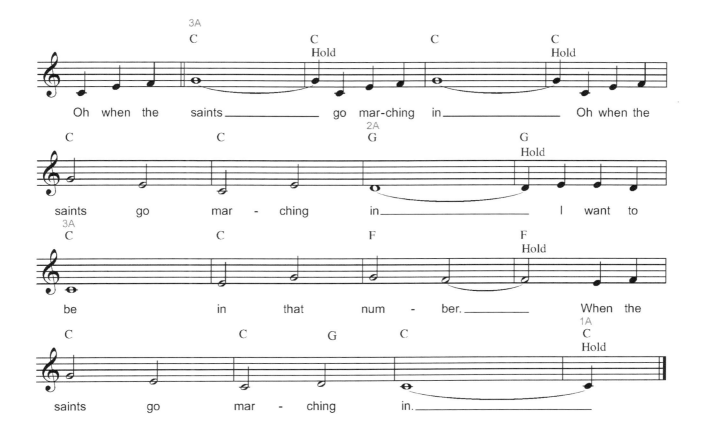

INSTANT PRACTICE METHOD:

Play each stage smoothly and confidently before you move on to the next step.

- (i) With your **right hand** in the C five-finger position, find the **melody notes**
- (ii) With your **left hand** in the C five-finger position, play the **bass notes**
- (iii) With both hands in the C five-finger position, play the melody and bass notes simultaneously
- (iv) Sing the melody and play the chords with the left hand

CHAPTER 5: MUSICAL TIMING

When you play songs that you already know, you play the timing of the notes from memory, so you don't have to concentrate on reading note values.
But it is useful to know something about musical timing for reasons that will become obvious as you proceed in your musical education.

RHYTHM

Wherever there is music, you will see people nodding their heads, tapping their feet and clapping out the beat, even if they don't know the tune or the lyrics.
That is because **rhythm is at the very root of all music**.

When you play your favorite songs, no-one will notice if you play a wrong melody note here or there, but everyone notices when the rhythm is off.

The Instant method will help you keep a steady rhythm in your playing.

INVOLVEMENT IN THE RHYTHM

Rhythm is innate in every human being. From the steady beating of our heart, to the steady rhythm of our walking, our talking, our performing, and our dancing – we all have rhythm. The trick is to harness the rhythm that's already there and use it to enhance our playing.

In the pages that follow you will learn how to "Instantly" read musical timing.
But first you should learn the best (Instant) way to keep time.

<u>Foot Tapping</u> is a habit you should adopt as soon as possible.

Whenever you listen to, sing, or play music you must tap your foot to keep the beat.

Remember, tapping the beat is not tapping out the melody.
The beat is that strong **1 2 3 4 pulse** that the bass drum in a band would typically play.

Start right away:

    Put on the radio or your favorite CD, or just think of a tune in your head.

    Listen to the beat, tap it out with your left foot (or your head) and do not stop until the song is over.

    Remember to tap every time you listen to music or count out beats for any reason.

TIP: *When tapping, you don't have to lift your whole foot on each beat. Lift either your heel or the front part of your foot and bring down that part on each beat. Each person will find what is comfortable for them – but the main thing is to do it!*

HOW TO COUNT IN MUSIC

Counting and foot tapping must always be even.

There should be no hesitation because you are looking for a melody note.

Play more slowly if you are unsure of the notes, but keep the rhythm steady.
It is better to find the notes first and practice the pattern of the tune before you try to play the time values.

Counting and foot tapping happen simultaneously.

Counting a note's value starts from the moment you sound the note.
You play the note, count "one" and tap your foot at the same time.
The note is held down for the entire amount of its time value.

Next you will learn note values and how they fit into the tapping and counting.

NOTE VALUES

Note values are part of the rhythm of a song.

When you listen to songs, you will notice that, while the even beat is always the same, some parts of the melodies are short and fast, others are slow and some notes are held for longer than others.

The shape of a note denotes its time value.

To the right is a diagram giving you an overview **of some musical notes, their time values and their names.**

You only have to know a few of them for the Instant method, but it is worthwhile having this as a reference for future studies.

Whole Note	𝅝	4 Counts
Half Note	𝅗𝅥	2 Counts
Quarter Note	♩	1 Count
2 Eighth Notes	♫	1 Count
4 Sixteenth Notes	♬♬	1 Count
8 Thirty-second Notes		1 Count

THE QUARTER NOTE

Each quarter note gets one beat, one count and one foot tap. Give it a try.

(i)   Keep an even beat with your foot and say "one" for each quarter note.

(ii)   Clap or play the quarter notes, counting aloud and tapping your foot.

TIP: *Give yourself four steady foot taps before you begin.*

Quarter Notes:	♩	♩	♩	♩	♩	♩	♩	♩
Count:	1	1	1	1	1	1	1	1

THE HALF NOTE

The Half note lasts for 2 counts.

To play half notes, you strike the note and tap your foot as you say "one."
You hold the note down while you tap your foot and say "two."
Note that each half note is only played once and then held for the rest of the time that the foot taps.

(i)   Try counting the half notes below, remembering to keep a steady beat with your foot tapping.

(ii)   Clap or play the same line, tapping your foot on every count (even when you are not striking a note).

TIP: *Before you start to play the notes, give yourself a <u>slow,</u> steady four counts to "count yourself in"*

Half Notes:	𝅗𝅥		𝅗𝅥		𝅗𝅥		𝅗𝅥	
Count:	1	2	1	2	1	2	1	2

(iii) This is a mixture of half notes and quarter notes
Practice tapping, counting, clapping and then playing these notes.

Now go back to your songs and look at the timing. Count the notes, tap your foot, and notice if they are held for one or two beats.

BARS OR MEASURES

Take a look at the songs you have just played.

The staff is divided by vertical lines called bar lines.

These "bar lines" divide the music into "bars."

Double bar lines indicate the end of a song or section.

"BARS" AND "MEASURES" MEAN EXACTLY THE SAME THING. WE SAY "BARS."

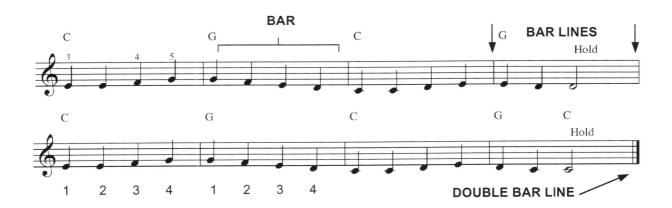

Each bar contains an equal number of beats. To test this statement:

(i) Count the beats in each bar of "Ode to Joy." There are 4 beats.

(ii) Now count the beats in each bar of "Merrily We Roll Along". Even though the values of the notes are different, there are also 4 beats in each bar.

(iii) Count the beats in "Lightly Row." There are 4 beats in each bar.

TIME SIGNATURES

If you go back and look at the beginning of each of your songs, you will see that after the Treble clef, there is a fraction, 4/4.

This fraction is called a **Time Signature**.
The 4/4 means that there are 4 quarter notes in each bar.

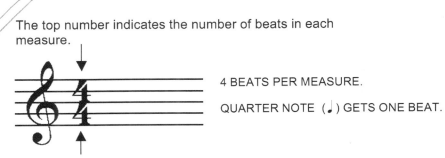

The time signature 4/4 ("four, four") may also be written as 𝄴 ("Common Time").

Now go back to your songs and this time when you count, instead of counting the values of single notes, you can count in fours for each bar, saying and tapping
"**1 2 3 4 | 1 2 3 4**" as you play the melodies.

Below are excerpts from 3 songs with the counts written below the notes.

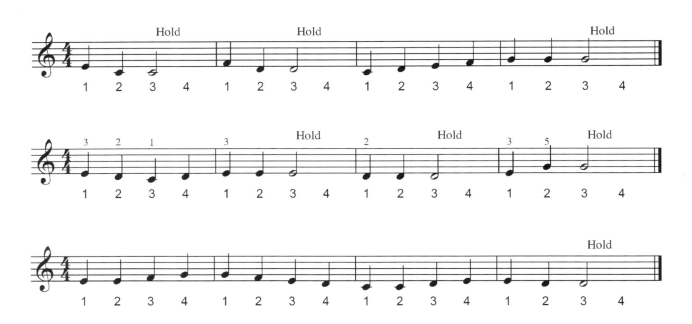

72

3/4 - A NEW TIME SIGNATURE – A NEW SONG

3 BEATS PER MEASURE.

QUARTER NOTE (♩) GETS ONE BEAT.

Below is the old favorite, "Beautiful Brown Eyes." Have fun with it.

(i)   Play the melody notes with your right hand in the C five-finger position.

(ii) Play the bass notes with your left hand in the C five-finger position.

(iii) To play the chords, your left hand changes from the C to the F and the G positions.

(iv) Count the beats in the bars. There are 3. See the 3/4 time signature? *3/4 time is also known as "Waltz time".*

"BEAUTIFUL BROWN EYES"

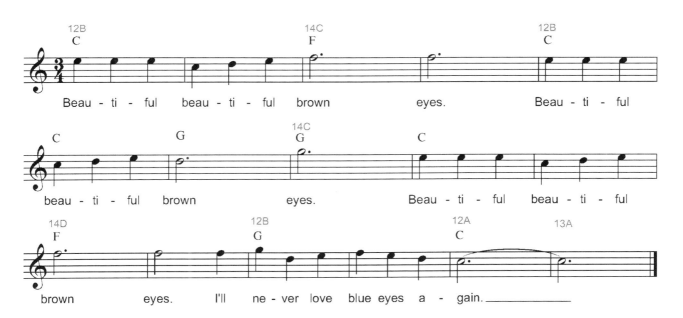

Did you notice the half note with a dot after it in this song?

When that note is in a bar in 3/4 time, it is the only note in that bar.
So you can deduce that the **time value of the dotted half note is 3 beats**.

THE DOTTED HALF NOTE

Play the note and tap your foot on the count of "one."
Continue to hold the note while you tap your foot on "two" and on "three".

There's a general musical rule you can learn from the dotted half note:
A dot after a note increases a note by half its time value.

Think of the dot as shorthand for the phrase "plus half again."

Here's how it works:

The value of the half note is 2 beats   **1 2 + 1 = 3 beats**
Remember this rule – you'll need it later.

Apart from dots, there is **another musical symbol that lengthens the time value** of notes. This is the **Tie**.

TIED NOTES

Look at the F note in the fourth bar of "Beautiful Brown Eyes."
It is linked to the previous F note by a curved line. This curved line is called a **TIE.**

When two notes on the same line or space are tied to each other, the first note is played and the second note is held. So a "tie" lengthens the first note's value by the time value of the second note.

In the "Beautiful Brown Eyes" example, you **play the first F**, holding it for three counts and you **continue to hold down the tied F note** while counting and tapping another "one, two, three".

Below are the first four bars of "Beautiful Brown Eyes" for reference:

Play "Beautiful Brown Eyes" again, tapping and playing, being aware of the counting.
Then try "Saints" again – there are some new things to learn.

"WHEN THE SAINTS GO MARCHING IN"

(i) Work out the melody. Notice the tied notes.

(ii) Work out the chords. Notice that there are not chord symbols above *every* bar. That's because **chord symbols that apply to several bars following each other only have to be written once**.

For clarity some composers write the chord symbol at the beginning of each line even if it is the same chord as the previous bar. After a chord is played, you stay on the same chord until a new chord symbol appears.

(iii) Have fun singing along with your playing.

Once you feel confident playing the timing of this song from memory, you should take note of the written timing because there are some new things to learn.

THE WHOLE NOTE

Did you notice the new type of note in the second bar? That's a "whole note."
When a whole note is in a bar of 4/4 time, it is the only note in that bar.
So you can deduce that the **time value of a whole note is 4 beats**.

HOW TO PLAY AND COUNT THE WHOLE NOTE:

Play the note and tap your foot on the count of "one."

Continue to hold the note while you tap your foot on "two", "three" and "four."

(ii) Sing the melody, tapping your foot and counting.

(iii) Play the song, being aware of the counting.

PICK UP NOTES

Did you notice that there are three beats instead of four in the first bar of ~~this song~~? No, it's not a mistake – **melodies don't always start with the first beat of a bar**. We call those odd numbers of notes **PICK UP NOTES**.

HOW TO COUNT AND PLAY PICKUP NOTES:

To count the pick-up notes first establish a steady beat by counting a bar of 4/4 aloud. This is often referred to as a "bar of nothing". The next four counts will be the pick-up bar. Beats **2**, **3** and **4** are the pick-up notes that are played.

Here is a count chart to help you:

"1   2   3   4 | 1   **2   3   4**"
   (silent count) | (silent) **play play play**

You should be **tapping your foot on every count**, including the tied notes.

This is how it should sound when you sing and count:

"*(1 2 3 4)* *(1)* **Oh when the saints** *(2 3 4)* *(1)* **Go march-ing in** *(2 3 4)* *(1)*

Oh when the saints *(2)* **go** *(4)* **march-** *(2)* **ing** *(4)* **in** *(2 3 4 1)*" and so on.

Note that, because rhythm has to be equal and balanced in music, the **number of counts in the final bar is shortened** by the number of beats in the first bar.

Since the song began on the second beat in 4/4 time, the last bar only contains 1 beat. Adding up the first and the last bar equals four beats.

Many songs begin with pick up notes. "Happy Birthday" and "Star Spangled Banner" are just two examples.

Practice "When the Saints Go Marching In" being aware of the timing of both the whole notes and the pick up notes.

"JINGLE BELLS"

Play "Jingle Bells" again. This version has a new note value – the eighth note.

THE EIGHTH NOTE

A single eighth note looks like this:

Two eighth notes can be joined like this:

Or they can be written separately like this:

There are two eighth notes in a quarter note.
They are **exactly even in time.**

HOW TO PLAY AND COUNT EIGHTH NOTES:

When you tap your foot while you count, the quarter note count is on the "down beat".

Your foot goes down to tap each time you count "one" "two" "three" "four."

1   2   3   4

Did you notice that, between the down beats, you have to lift your foot up so you can tap again. Try it. There are two foot movements to each count – **the down beats and the up beats.**

Eighth notes are played on both the down beat and the up beat because there are **two eighth notes to one** (quarter note) **beat**.

You count "one" on the down beat and count "and" on the up beat.

Like this:

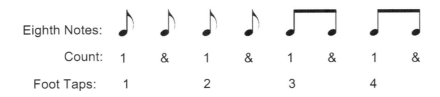

Practice this exercise, remembering to keep a steady beat while tapping your foot and counting aloud. You can either play notes or clap, or even tap your hand on any surface to make a sound on the eighth notes.

Practice counting and playing eighth notes until you feel confident.

> ***TIP:*** *Even if the eighth notes are only in one section of the song, count in eighth notes as much as possible.*
> *For example you would count "1 & 2 & 3 & 4 &." instead of "1 2 3 4".*

These exercises will help you keep an even beat by tapping your foot and counting.

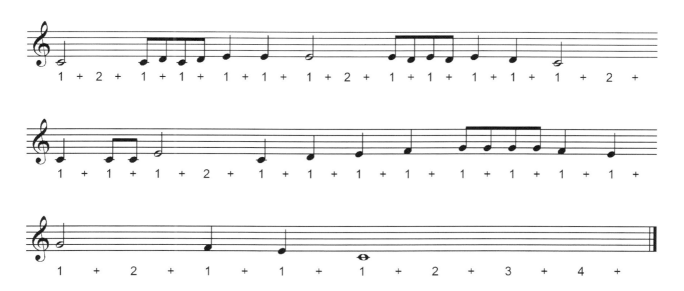

Here's practice counting in 4/4 time:

THE DOTTED QUARTER NOTE

In "Jingle Bells" when you sing: "Jingle all the way," you pause slightly on "all" and make "the" a very short note. That **skipping type rhythm** with a longer and a shorter note is written as a **dotted quarter note followed by an eighth note**.

Look at the third bar of "Jingle Bells" ("jin - gle all the – ") to find a dotted quarter note (on "all") followed by a single eighth note (on "the").

Remember that a **dot after a note increases a note by half its time value**.

This is how to work it out:

The value of the quarter note is 1 beat + the dot is 1/2 beat = 1 and ½ beat. The eighth note follows. A dotted quarter note plus one eighth note equals 2 beats.

Think in eighth notes:

Count like this: 1   &   2   &

"JINGLE BELLS"

Play "Jingle Bells" counting and tapping your foot.

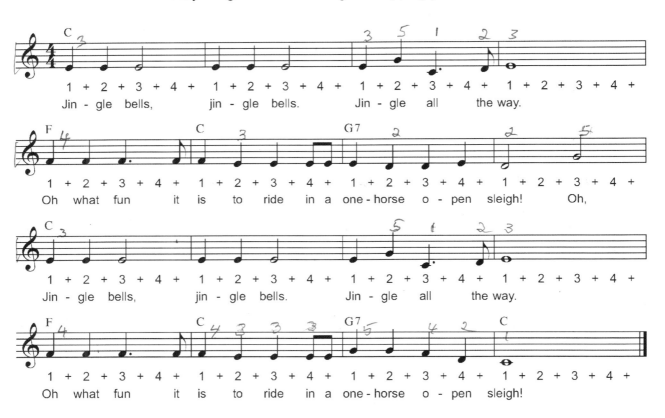

Foot-taps: The eighth note following the dotted quarter note is on an up beat (when you lift your foot and count "and").

Congratulations! You now know most of the timing you're going to need to play all the songs in this "Instant" course!

CHAPTER 6: MOVING AROUND THE KEYBOARD

There are a limited number of songs that only use the 5 notes in the
five-finger hand position, so if you want to increase your repertoire,
it's time to extend your hand out of the five-finger position.

EXTENDING THE C FIVE-FINGER POSITION

Begin by going just **one note down** from the C five-finger position.

In the next song ("Mary-Anne") you will play the **B below middle C** with the first finger of your right hand.

(i)   First find the notes with your right hand in the C five-finger position.

       FINGERING: The first five notes of the song are notes of the C major chord.
       You play them with fingers 1, 3 and 5. The next two notes are played with fingers 2
       and 4; then only finger 1 stretches out of the C five-finger position to play the note
       B, one step below C.

(ii)   Make sure you have the timing correct. Tap your foot and count.
       Don't forget the tied notes at the end of each line.

(iii)   There are only two chords - C and G.

"MARY-ANNE"

© 2011 Charles Segal Publications, 16 Grace Rd. Ste 1, Newton, MA 02459

81

This next song goes one note upwards out of the C five-finger position to play the note A.

You can use any fingering you prefer, but suggested finger numbers are written next to the notes.

You will notice how the flexibility of the first finger makes it easy to stretch out of position.

Try it!

"TWINKLE TWINKLE"

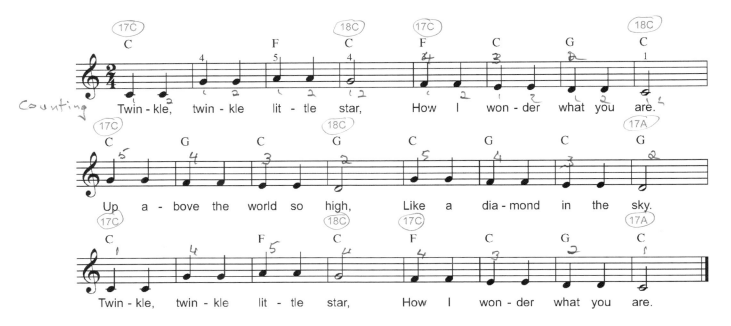

There are three chords – C, F, and G. Your left hand stays in the C five-finger position to play the bass notes and moves to the F and G five-finger positions to play the chords.

2/4 TIME SIGNATURE

Did you notice the new time signature at the beginning of "Twinkle Twinkle?"

2/4 means that there are **two quarter note beats in each bar**.

How to Count 2/4 Time:

You count: "**one two, one two, one two, one two,**" instead of the "one two three four" of 4/4 time.

The new time signature does not change the value of any notes – just the way you count.

MOVING BETWEEN TWO HAND POSITIONS

The next song, "On Top of Old Smoky," will give you practice extending your hands further on the keyboard without losing your place.

The melody moves between the C five-finger position and the F five-finger position.

Go through the exercises below first and you will see how much easier it will be to play the melody.

(i) With your right hand in the C position, play a C major chord, first as a broken chord – C E G – and then all three notes played together.

(ii) Play middle C with your first finger, and top C with your fifth finger – an octave higher. Play them separately and then together.

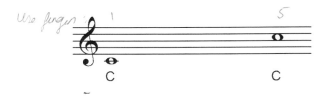

(iii) Now fill in the two missing notes of the C major chord (E and G) with your second and third fingers. Play a broken C major chord again, but this time add the top note of the chord. The broken chord will be C E G C.

When you break up an extended chord for 4 or more notes, it is called an **ARPEGGIO.**

(iv) Change to the F five-finger position and play an F major broken chord (F A C). Now play the F major chord.

Notice that the same C note is played by your fifth finger in the F chord as in the four noted C chord.

(v) Practice going between C and F this way:

(a) Play a C major arpeggio (C E G C)
(b) When you get to the top C, hold it down then contract your hand out of the stretch. You will automatically be in the F five-finger position.
(c) Play the F and A notes of an F major chord together (so you sound F A C)

You have just smoothly and easily shifted your hand position from extended C position to the F five-finger position. Practice this until you feel confident.

Now look at the music of "On Top of Old Smoky" below.

Notice that when you are aware of the C and F hand positions, it is much easier to find the notes.

Bars 1 – 3 are in the C extended position.

Bars 3 – 7 are in the F five-finger position.

During the pause of the tied notes you move back into the C position and repeat the whole process again.

"AULD LANG SYNE"

Notice that in quite a few places there are several notes played for just one word (like: "o – o – auld lang syne").

The line that joins those notes is not a tied note; it is a **SLUR.**

A slur joins two or more notes, indicating that they are to be played smoothly or legato.
For example, in the second to last measure there is a slur from C to A.
When playing the "A" use a light touch so as not to overemphasize the attack of the note.
The following "G" should be played with a normal attack.

Also notice that often the lyrics will have a dash under the notes to show the word is being stretched across several notes.

Notice the pick up note. Here's a guide on the counting:

```
        Should | old    ac-quain-tance | be      for – got  and -
(1 2 3)   4    | 1 & 2   &  3 & 4 &    | 1&  2    &   3&  4 &
```

INVERSIONS

C, F, and G major chords are found in most songs in the key of C.

Practice going from a C major to an F major chord and then from a C major to a G major chord.

Notice that **you have to lift your whole hand** to move to the new position.

When you pick up and move your whole hand, two things can happen:

(1)   you lose your place and hit a wrong note or chord unless you look carefully at your hands
(2)   your ~~accompaniment does~~ not sound smooth and connected
        Playing

The INSTANT way to solve this is to play "<u>Chord Inversions.</u>"

Chord inversions are when all the notes of a chord are played, but not in the usual order of 1st (root), 3rd and 5th. You will instead "invert" the note order.

The C major chord can be played in **root position**:

Or in **first inversion**:

← this means E is the bottom note of the chord.

Or in **second inversion**:

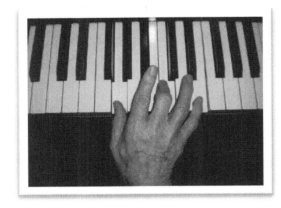

You can even play a C major chord like this:

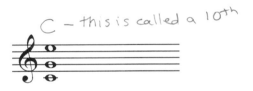

If you can't play all the notes simultaneously, play a broken chord or play C and G in the left hand and E in the right hand. It is still a C major chord.

As long as the three chord notes, C, E and G are played, it does not matter which position the notes are in, it still remains a C major chord.

(ii) Practice playing a C major chord in the inversions shown above.

(iii) Experiment with your own inversions of C major.

INVERSIONS MAKE PLAYING CHORDS EASIER

The trick is to play the chords in inversions that make it easy to go from one chord to the other without having to lift your whole hand. Here's an example:

(i) **Play a C major chord and then a G major chord in their root positions.**
This is a big jump!

If you look carefully at the notes of the C and G major chords, you'll notice that the **G note appears in both chords.**

When this happens, you can keep your finger on that common note (G) and play the closest notes of the next chord.

The other notes of the G major chord are B and D – notes next door to C and E, the first two notes of the C major chord. It is easy to move fingers 1 and 2 down one note.

Playing major chords this way gives your playing a smooth, connected sound.

A chord symbol with a slash shows which note to play on the bottom of the chord.

G/B = B is on the bottom
C/G = G is on the bottom

(ii) Now **start on a G major chord and go to a C major chord.** Try it this way:

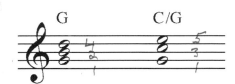

(iii) **Practice all the ways you can transition between a C and G major chord without lifting your hand and jumping around.**

GOING FROM C MAJOR TO F MAJOR

(i) Play an F major chord in its root position, first and second inversions.

(ii) See if you can work out the easiest way to move between a C and F major chord using inversions.

Hint: Start by seeing if they have any common notes!

CHORD PRACTICE

(i) If you want to really improve your chord playing, you can practice going all the way up the keyboard, playing a C major chord in all its inversions.

(ii) Do this with the right and the left hand. Then do the same going downwards. You can also practice the inversions playing broken chords.

(iii) Try the same exercise with a G major chord and an F major chord.

Go back and play all the songs you have learned, using inversions to make the chord transitions easier.

BONUS PRACTICE

The next two well-known pieces will give you an opportunity to practice **extended hand positions** for the melody and **chord inversions** in both hands.

Can you see how many of the **melody notes are chord notes** written in different inversions?

Notice the dotted quarter notes and pick-up notes.

For the chord symbol, G7, just play a regular G major chord for now.
You will learn about seventh chords later on.

- In the first line of "Brahms Lullaby" the counts are written under the notes to help you with the dotted notes. Before you try to play the notes, clap out the timing.
- For the second line of music, you write the counts under the notes. (timing, counting aloud "one and two and...." etc.)

"BRAHMS LULLABY"

"SILENT NIGHT"

Now play the famous marching song below. It's great practice for the extended hand positions in the right hand and chord inversions in the left hand.

You probably know the rhythm of the melody from memory, but when you read the music, will notice the new note value in this song – the **DOTTED EIGHTH NOTE.** Don't be alarmed—all dotted notes work the same way: the dotted note is longer by half. Until you learn the details, play the rhythm the Instant way: Hold the dotted note longer and shorten the next note. That will give a kind of skipping rhythm to the song.

INSTANT SHARPS, FLATS, AND NATURALS

Sharps and **Flats** raise or lower the pitch of the note.
A **Natural** cancels a sharp or flat.

KEY SIGNATURES

You may see Sharps or Flats placed on particular lines or spaces after the clef at the beginning of a musical staff.
These are part of the "**key signature**," telling you what key a piece is in.
A sharp or flat in a **key signature affects every note of that name in the** ~~piece~~ song.

Accidentals are Sharps, Flats and **Naturals** sometimes found in a ~~piece~~ song at the left side of the ~~head of a~~ note. These are called accidentals because "they do not happen naturally" in the particular key that you are in.
Accidentals only last for the bar in which they appear.
The bar line automatically "erases" them. *after the accidentals*

You won't see a key signature in this Instant course, *(except in the Bonus Section)* because all the songs are in the key of C, which has no sharps or flats. But you may find accidentals in some songs in C.
When you see a sharp or flat in the key of C, you know that you have to **play a black note**.

INSTANT SHARPS AND FLATS

There is a ~~slow~~ *detailed* explanation about sharps and flats, but the "Instant" version is all you need at this stage.

<u>**This is a Sharp:**</u> ♯   **A sharp raises the pitch** of a note.

When a sharp appears in front of a note, **play the black note to the right**.

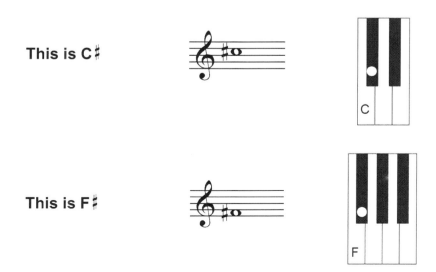

This is C♯

This is F♯

This is a Flat: ♭   A flat lowers the pitch of a note.

When a flat appears in front of a note, **play the black note to the left**.

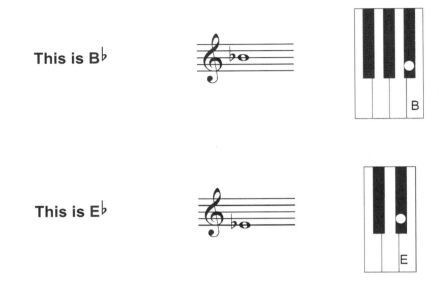

This is a Natural: ♮   A natural in front of a note returns the note to its original pitch.

A natural assumes there was an accidental in front of that note previously.

In the example below, you will see how the first F is sharp, (black note), but the second one has a natural sign, making it the original F note (white note).

Like other **accidentals**, a natural affects the note it precedes and all subsequent notes of the same name for **that one bar only**.

In the two bar exercise below, The first and second F's in Bar 1 are F#'s. The bar line cancels the #, so the F in Bar 2 is the white note, F.

SAME NOTE, DIFFERENT NAME

Each black note has the possibility of being called two names because it has white notes on either side.

For example, C♯ can also be called D♭. These are called "**enharmonic**" notes because they are different in name only. "Enharmonic change" is another phrase describing this.

The following diagram shows the enharmonic names for the black keys:

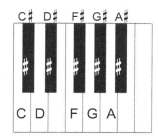 OR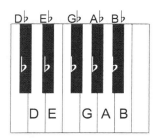

"FRANKIE AND JOHNNY"

Notice the E♭ accidental in bar 8. To play an E♭ simply play the black note to the left of the E. Remember: the bar line cancels an accidental so the E in bar 11 is a white note.

The C7 chord is C, E, G and B♭, but you can just play a regular C major triad if you prefer. That is, C E G.

CHAPTER 7: CHORDS

Reformat

Since all of the songs in this Instant course are in the key of C, it is not necessary to get bogged down in explaining scales and chords. Scales and chords are interesting and will definitely advance your education and enjoyment of music when you are ready for them, but, at this stage, you will be able to play just as well learning the chords the Instant way.

If you see a chord symbol that you're not sure of, you can just play the letter name of the chord as a bass note. Sometimes the 1 and 5 chord notes will sound good together. Experiment and have fun!

MORE CHORDS – INSTANTLY   **G7**

When playing your songs in the key of C major on all the white notes, you will sometimes notice a "7" after a chord symbol – most likely a "G7." This is called a seventh chord.

A "7" in a chord symbol indicates that the seventh note of the scale should be added to the chord. **Count up seven white keys from G** and play that F note as part of the chord.

So the notes of G7 are G B D F

 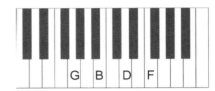

An easy way to play G7 is to play the F and G notes next to each other.

 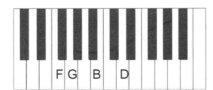

Many pianists play only three notes for G7 – B F G

 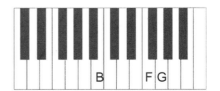

A G7 chord may sound strange to you at first, but it **sounds great right before going to a C major chord** – try it. Play G7 C a few times.

Am Em Dm

A small "m" after a letter denotes a minor chord.

When you're playing **in the key of C** major (on all the white keys), the chords formed by playing the first, third and fifth notes starting on **C, F and G are automatically major chords.**

D, E and A are automatically minor chords.

Play fingers 1, 3 and 5 starting on C and going up the keyboard, making a chord on each white note until you get to A.

You will be playing these chords:

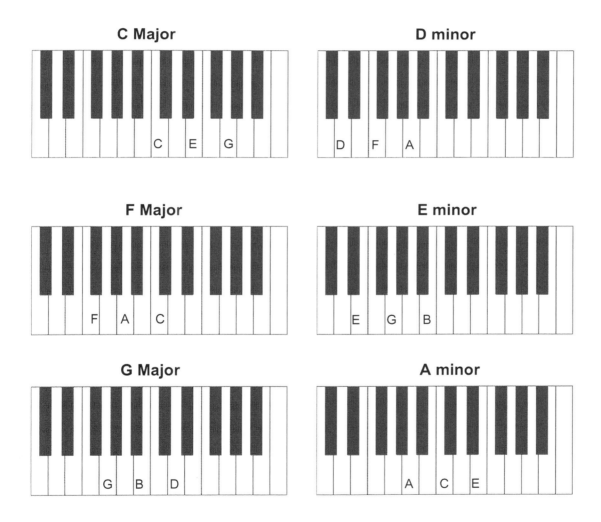

Do you hear the **subtle difference** between the major and minor chords?
Major chords are said to sound "happy" and minor chords, "sad."

The chord on B is more complicated – It's a B diminished chord

B diminished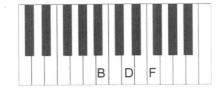

MAJOR OR MINOR - INSTANTLY

The difference between a major and minor chord is the third, or middle note.
A chord is comprised of notes 1, 3 and 5 of a scale. So the "middle" note of a chord in root position is the third note of the scale.

The **minor has a ~~flat~~ flattened** (lowered) **middle note** (third) making it sound sad.

(I) Play a C major chord (C E G).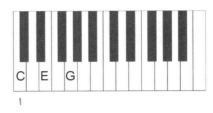

(ii) Play a C major chord with a ~~flat~~ flattened third. (E becomes E♭). This is a C minor chord. Hear the difference?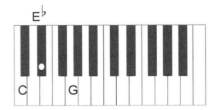

A major chord can easily become a minor chord.
Using that theory, you can also **make a minor chord into a major chord**.
If the third sounds sad, simply **sharpen** it (raise it one half step).

(iii) Play an Am (A minor) chord (A C E)

(iv)   Play Am then ~~sharp~~ *sharpen* the third note
       (C becomes C♯)

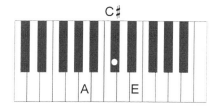

When you see the chord symbols A, D or E in the key of C major you know that they are minor chords played on all white keys. So all you have to do to make them major is sharp*en* the third by playing the black note to the right.

(v)   Play A minor and then A major

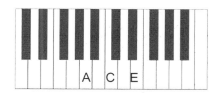 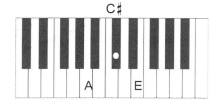

Play D minor and then D major

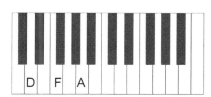 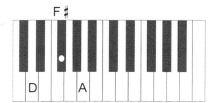

Play E minor and then E major

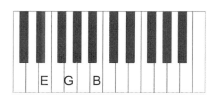 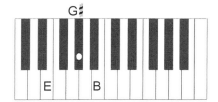

"STAR-SPANGLED BANNER"

Watch out for the accidentals - the F# black note to the right of F.
Notice the extended hand positions - the finger numbers should help.
Here's an opportunity to find new chords the Instant way.

The ⌢ symbol is a **pause sign or "FERMATA."** There are three in the last line.
A fermata has no particular time value – just pause as long as you feel is right.

"YELLOW ROSE OF TEXAS"

This song has lots of practice for inversions and extended hand positions.

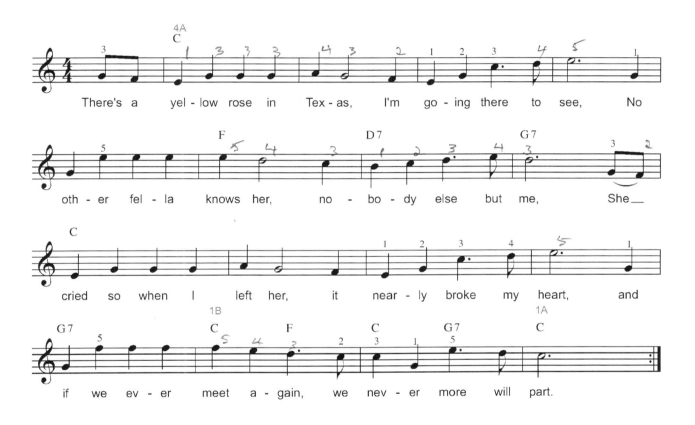

*Kayla please
Add a line:
CHORD SHORTCUTS:
For G7 play BFG
For A7 play C#GA
For D7 play F#CD
Use left hand fingers
5 2 1

"CARELESS LOVE"

This is a slow song with good examples of broken chords in the melody line.
Notice the chord challenges: G7, A7, D7 and F to Fm.
Remember, the 7th note is just one white note down from the chord name.
To make it easier you could just play the bass note or only two chord notes.

CHORD SHORTCUTS:

"AMAZING GRACE"

8vb means that you play an **octave lower** than written.
Notice how many of the melody notes are chord notes
There are slurs and tied notes – be careful!

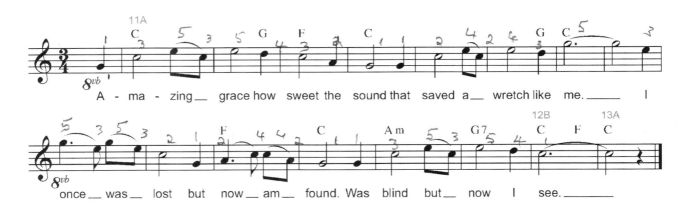

"HAVA NAGILAH"

This lively song is in the key of **A minor** – a relative key of **C major**,
so it also has **no sharps or flats in the key signature**.
There are **sharps in front of all the G notes**, so look out for them!
Notice the **E chord** (E G# B)
For **E7** (E G# B D) you can play a bass note or G# D E

The "**rest**" sign in the third to last bar of the song indicates silence for the whole bar. You count "1 2 3 4" but don't play.

The extra bar-lines with dots are **repeat signs**, explained on page 108.

D.C. al Fine at the end of the song means that you **repeat the whole song from the beginning to the end**.

PLAYING SCALES FOR FINGER EXERCISE

Don't panic – we're not going to make you play lots of scales – just the C major scale. Knowing scale fingering will help you play some melodies that stretch across the keyboard.

Playing scales is also a good way to give your mind a break from playing songs. Like standing up and stretching at intermission when you're at a show or game.

In the playing by ear section ("Getting Acquainted with Sound") we played some scales. You can go over that section again now or just continue with this lesson. (Page 27-30)

PLAYING A C MAJOR SCALE WITH THE RIGHT HAND

A scale is a series of notes, usually within an octave, that begin and end on the same letter. Major scales have eight notes.

The C major scale is: **C D E F G A B C**

Try it!

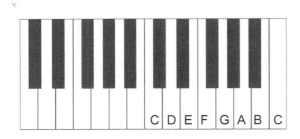
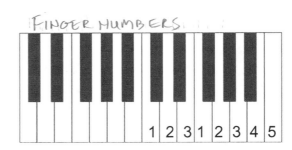

FINGER NUMBERS

To play the eight notes easily, you should use specific fingering.
It's simple math, really – **3 fingers + 5 fingers** = 8 piano keys in a scale.

The order of the fingers in many scales is: 1 2 3 - 1 2 3 4 5

104

And in reverse: 5 4 3 2 1 - 3 2 1

(i) Put your **right hand in** the **C five-finger position** with your first finger on Middle C.

(ii) Play the first three fingers – 1 2 3 (C D E).

(iii) After you have played the 3rd finger, the next key up (F) is played with the 1st finger again. So, just **tuck your thumb under your third finger** and press down the next key to the right (F) with your thumb (first finger).

(iv) When you reach the 8th key with your 5th finger (C), proceed back down the scale again, playing fingers 4 3 2 1.

(v) After you have played down to the 1st finger, **swing the 3rd finger over the thumb** to play the next white key to the left (E). Continue down to C.

You have just played the C Major Scale!

PLAYING THE C MAJOR SCALE WITH THE LEFT HAND

Your left hand also deserves a little limbering up – so here goes:

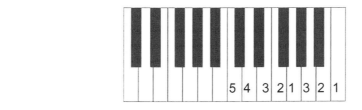

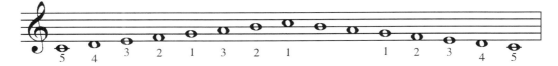

(i) Put your **left hand in the C five-finger position with your fifth finger on low C**.

(ii) Play fingers 5 4 3 2 1 (C D E F G).

(iii) The next key up is played with finger 3. Just **swing your third finger over your thumb and play the next key up** to your right (A).

(iv)   Play fingers 3 2 1, reaching Middle C.

(v)   Proceed back down the scale again, playing fingers 1 2 and 3 (C B A).

(vi)   **After you have played the 3rd finger, tuck the 1st finger under the third to play the next white key down (to the left) (G).**

(vii)   Play fingers 1 2 3 4 5, playing back down to lower C

You have just played the C Major scale with your left hand!

Play these scales whenever you fingers and your mind need a "stretch.

"YANKEE DOODLE DANDY"

This song will give you the opportunity to try out your scale fingering.
You'll need to swing the 3rd finger over the thumb in bars 7 and 11.
Keep an eye out for the other suggested fingering next to the notes.
Notice the 2/4 time signature.

"SHE'LL BE COMIN' 'ROUND THE MOUNTAIN"

Notice the pick-up notes in the first bar on "four and."

"AMERICA THE BEAUTIFUL"

Here's another song where you have to watch the fingering.
Notice the dotted quarter notes and the pick up note.

CHAPTER 8: MORE SIGNS & SYMBOLS

REPEAT SIGNS

Repeat Signs tell you to play the same musical passage more than once.
The signs are mainly used to save space. They also make reading music easier.

Repeat Sign = a double bar line with two dots

This left-facing sign tells us to **return to the right-facing sign** and repeat the music between the two signs. If there is no right-facing sign, repeat from the beginning.

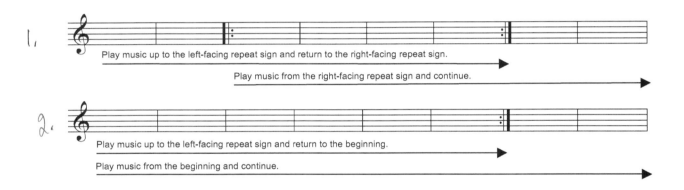

FIRST AND SECOND TIME BARS

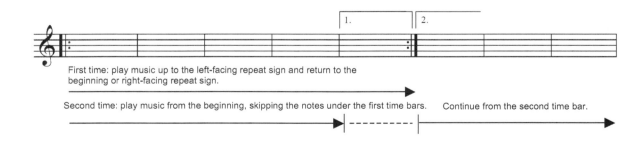

D.S. or Dal Segno means "Go back and repeat from this sign" 𝄋

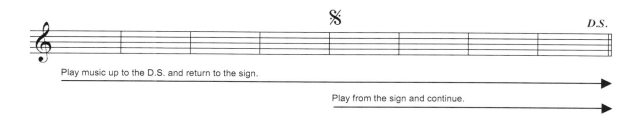

al Coda or **To Coda** means "go to the Coda".

The Coda (tail) is an extra few bars added to the end of the music.

The Coda is marked by this sign ⊕

D.S. al Coda means go back to the sign 𝄋
and repeat until you come to "al Coda" (or "to Coda"), then go to the Coda ⊕

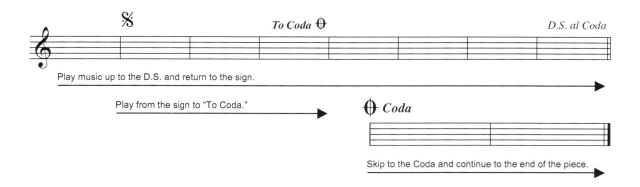

RESTS

When a composer wants silences in his song, he uses a **rest symbol**.
Rests have time values that correspond to note values.
When you see a rest in a song, you **lift your fingers off the keyboard** as you **count the beats for the rest**.

The following diagram illustrates notes and their corresponding rests.

WHOLE NOTE	𝅝	=	▬	WHOLE REST
HALF NOTE	𝅗𝅥	=	▬	HALF REST
QUARTER NOTE	♩	=	𝄽	QUARTER REST
EIGHTH NOTE	♪	=	𝄾	EIGHTH REST

Here are examples of the rests on the staff in 4/4 time. The counts are written in.

Rests always have the same position on the staff, in either clef.

The whole and the half rests look similar. The 4-count rest is higher (placed in the third space) than the 2-count rest.
To remember, use a balloon analogy – more air (value) floats higher.

Practice counting and playing the bars below.
Remember to lift your fingers off the keyboard for the rests.

Now go back through all of the songs and see if you recognize the rests.

"FUR ELISE"

We've all wanted to play "Fur Elise" at some stage of our lives.
Here's your chance to play it the "Instant" way.
This piece has two accidentals: the D# in the famous motif that starts the melody;
and the G# in all the bars that have the E chord.
Notice the natural that cancels out the D# on the third D of the motif.
If you practice your chord inversions, you should have no problem playing
this piece – notice all the chord notes that make up the melody.

"MOZART'S SONATA NO. 15"

This is a great piece to demonstrate chords and scales in a melody.
Have fun and watch the fingering carefully.
Notice the accidentals (F# and F natural) near the end

Notice that on the upward moving scales you tuck your thumb under after the third finger, but, moving downwards, you need an extra finger to play all the notes, so you **swing your fourth finger over your thumb** (instead of the third, as we do in most scales).

"BLUE DANUBE"

This famous waltz is a good example of how melodies are composed from arpeggios and chord inversions. See if you can spot the chords in the melody. Notice the accidental near the end.

"AURA LEE"

A famous pop song, "Love Me Tender," is based on this melody.
In the first part of song your hand is in the G five-finger position.
In the second part your hand is in the C position until the stretch in the second to last bar.

"RED RIVER VALLEY"

This is a great song for practicing switching hand positions. The fingering will help.

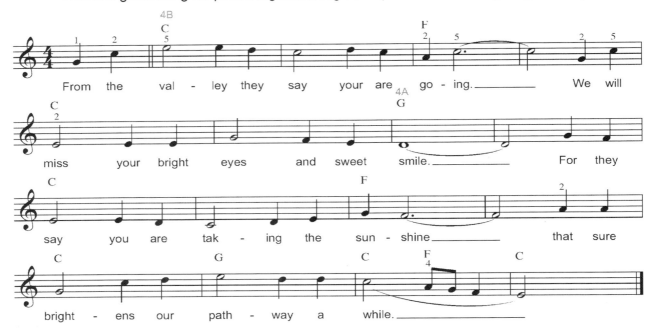

"HOME ON THE RANGE"

Watch out for the ledger lines in the melody – they go down to the G below middle C.
This is when chord inversions will come in handy to prevent your left hand
from getting entangled with your right hand playing the melody.

"THE OLD FOLKS AT HOME"
"Swanee River"

This song has repeat signs.
Notice the counts under the dotted notes and the rests.

115

A NEW TIME SIGNATURE: 6/8 TIME

THE TIME SIGNATURE FORMULA

There is a formula for reading the fractions in time signatures:

The **top number tells you how many beats** in each bar.

The **bottom number says what kind of beats** they are.

4/4	4 BEATS IN A BAR QUARTER NOTE BEATS	2/4	2 BEATS IN A BAR QUARTER NOTE BEATS
3/4	3 BEATS IN A BAR QUARTER NOTE BEATS	6/8	6 BEATS IN A BAR EIGHTH NOTE BEATS
12/8	12 BEATS IN A BAR EIGHTH NOTE BEATS		

COUNTING IN EIGHTH NOTES

In 4/4 time we counted 1 2 3 4 for each quarter note beat.

4/4 | 1 2 3 4 | 1 2 3 4 | 1 2 3 4 | 1 2 3 4 ||

In 6/8 time the **count is in eighth notes: 1 2 3 4 5 6**

6/8 | 1 2 3 4 5 6 | 1 2 3 4 5 6 | 1 2 3 4 5 6 ||

You have to think of the note values differently: ♪ = 1 beat

♩ = 2 beats

♩. = 3 beats

Here is an example of counting 3 bars with a 6/8 time signature:

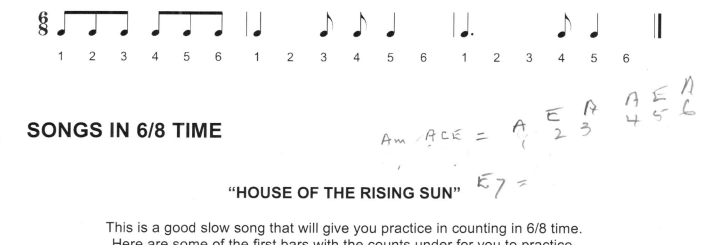

SONGS IN 6/8 TIME

"HOUSE OF THE RISING SUN"

This is a good slow song that will give you practice in counting in 6/8 time.
Here are some of the first bars with the counts under for you to practice.

© 2011 Charles Segal Publications, 16 Grace Rd. Ste 1, Newton, MA 02459

"WHEN JOHNNY COMES MARCHING HOME"

in 6/8 time

This song has a much faster-moving melody line.
Practice slowly until you can play all the melody notes easily.

Here are some of the first bars with the counts under for you to practice:

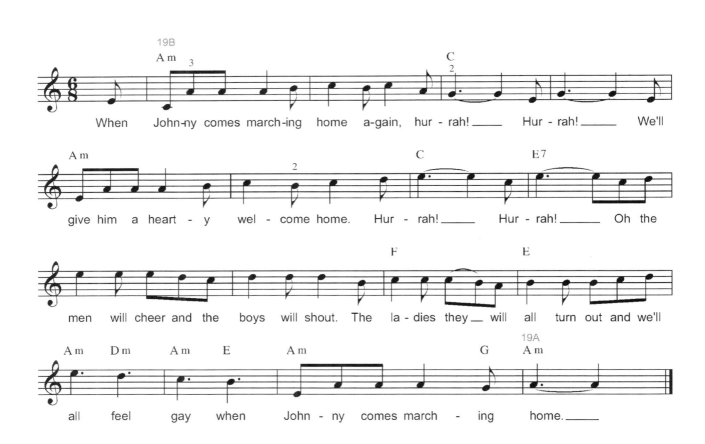

CHAPTER 9: LEFT HAND PATTERNS AND TECHNIQUES

Up to now, your left hand has played either one note in the bass or chords when you see a chord symbol. (↓ When you see a chord symbol) {RE-FORMAT} Once you are comfortable finding and playing major chords and inversions to accompany your melodies, you may feel like making the songs more interesting by doing more with your left hand. This chapter has some patterns to practice that can be used to accompany all of the songs in this book.

The accompaniment patterns are written in the bass clef.
If you don't want to learn the bass clef, you can always **refer to the keyboard diagrams** to find the notes and check the written music for the timing.

We suggest you take the extra time to become familiar with the names of the bass staff notes in case you should ever need to read them. On pages 128 and 129 you can see how songs/arrangements are written with both the Treble and Bass Staves. The Bass staff appears below the Treble staff with Middle C on a ledger line between them.

READING NOTES IN THE BASS CLEF – INSTANTLY

Here is a Bass staff with a Bass clef.

On the **Bass Staff** the **Five Lines** are: **G B D F A**

G B D F A

A good acronym to remember the names of the lines is: **G**ood **B**oys **D**eserve **F**un **A**lways

The **Four Spaces** in the **Bass Clef** are: **A C E G**

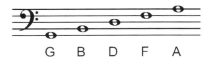

A C E G

A good acronym to remember the names of the spaces is: **A**ll **C**ows **E**at **G**rass

Middle C is positioned above the Bass staff and has its own ledger line.

An "Instant" way to remember the ~~Bass staff notes~~ *names of* Bass staff notes, is that they are positioned just one space or line down from the Treble staff notes.

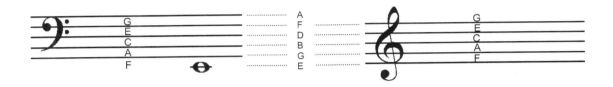

So if the **Treble** lines are: E G B D F
                                    | | | |
The **Bass** lines are: G B D F A → *shift a little to the right?*

It's the same with the spaces: Treble: **F A C E**
                                          | | |
                                 Bass: **A C E G**

On a line or space, the letters repeat, with "**F A C E**" starting on the last letter of "**E**very **G**ood **B**oy **D**eserves **F**un" and vice versa – like this:

E G B D **F A C E** G B D **F A C E** G B D **F A C E**... *and so on.*

EXERCISE:

Start at the bottom of the Bass staff (or even below it).

Count all the way up to the ledger lines above the Treble staff. Try it from the F space below the first Bass line. You can also ~~check~~ *try* it out on the keyboard, counting up in skips.

So, armed with all this knowledge, you shouldn't have any trouble finding a note on the Bass staff.

LEFT HAND WARM UP

You have already played chords and chord inversions with your left hand – so now you're going to see what those chords look like in written music.

C, F, ~~G~~ and G7 are ~~the most~~ common chords in songs in the key of C major.

This exercise will help you move between these chords in comfortable inversions.

Becoming proficient at this exercise will give you the motor skills to play the accompaniment patterns in C major, which can be transposed ~~later~~ to other keys, later.

Play these combinations:

(a) as straight chords
(b) as broken chords
(c) repeating each chord 4 times

Play each exercise at least 10 times.

For the keyboard diagrams:-
● = the position of the starting major chord
▨ = the position of the second chord

Practice TIP: Always practice difficult sections of songs separately before including them in the whole song. If a melody is tricky – just practice the right hand until you have it perfectly; if the chord changes are difficult – practice them alone first. This exercise is a good example you can follow to improve your technique for playing all the chords in this book.

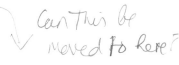

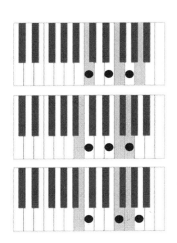

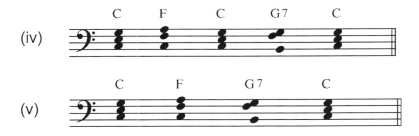

ACCOMPANIMENT PATTERNS

A good left hand accompaniment can add harmony and beat to your songs.
On the next few pages you will find many different accompaniment styles to choose from.

Audio examples of the accompaniment patterns ~~will be~~ are available for free on **CharlesSegal.com**

THE LAYOUT OF THE ACCOMPANIMENTS

There are five pages of accompaniments. (pages 123 – 127)
On pages 128 and 129 the patterns are written out in both treble and bass staves.
The patterns are shown mostly on a C major chord, except where we feel a chord change may need extra practice. On page 130 we show you how to transpose, so you can use the patterns for any chord.

Some of the patterns have variations marked "A B C D".
These are the same notes with different rhythmic patterns.

The patterns are shown with different time signatures, but once you gain experience, you will be able to vary any pattern to suit any time signature you may encounter.

Most of the patterns are repeated over two bars. But even if a pattern is only in one bar, you can repeat the bar as many times as you wish until you feel confident in your playing.

Some of the patterns have names and comments to help you in your selection.

SELECTING AN ACCOMPANIMENT PATTERN

You may have noticed that the songs in this book have a set of numbers and letters in grey above the chord symbols. These are suggestions for accompaniment patterns you can use to embellish the song.

Of course, once you become proficient at playing all the accompaniments, you can mix and match, choosing any patterns you prefer – and even create some of your own.

On page 128 there's an arrangement of the song, "Frankie and Johnny", written in the treble and bass staffs, which illustrates how you can put some simple patterns together to make a great arrangement.

When deciding which variations to play, bear this in mind:

When the melody is "busy" (with many notes) you can let the left hand be sparse – just play single chords. When there's a pause in the melody, you can fill in the gap with a busier left hand – like broken chords or rhythmic chords. Take a look at the arrangement of "Frankie and Johnny" for an example of how this works.

1. CHORDS ONLY

2. BROKEN CHORDS (ALBERTI BASS)

3. VAMPS

4. BASS MOVES FROM ROOT TO FIFTH

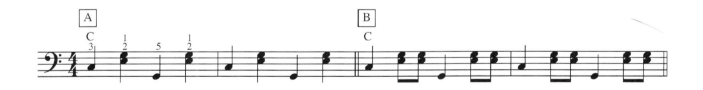

5. ROCK, BLUES OR BOOGIE

6. A: WALKING BASS   B: COUNTRY STYLE

7. A: ROCK VARIATION   B: WALKING BLUES / MARCHING BASS

8. A & B: SWING BASS   C: LATIN BEAT   D: JAZZ BEAT

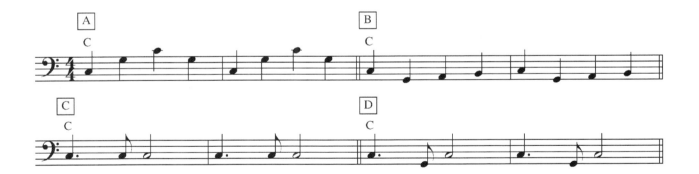

9. 3/4 TIME (YOU CAN HOLD THE BOTTOM NOTE)

10. JAZZ WALTZ

11. ROOT AND FIFTH IN EIGHTH NOTES

12. A: ARPEGGIOS

13. CHORDS IN 3/4

14. MORE VARIATIONS IN 3/4

15. CHORD CHANGES TO PRACTICE

16. CHORD CHANGES WITH FINGERING

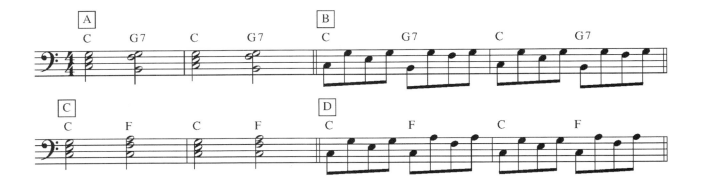

17. CHORDS IN 2/4 TIME

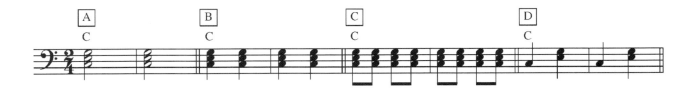

18. MORE 2/4 TIME

19. 6/8 TIME

20. TWO CHORD CHANGES IN A BAR

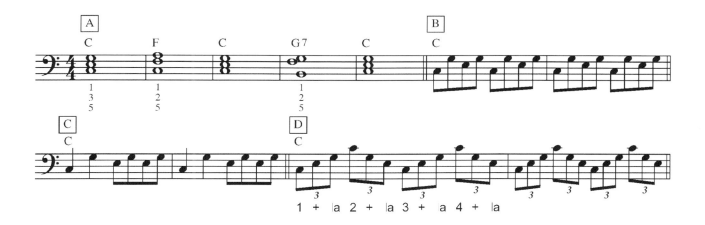

DEMO ARRANGEMENT OF "FRANKIE AND JOHNNY"

The arrangement is written in both staves to demonstrate how the patterns fit in.
The pattern numbers are written under the bass staff where they are being played.
Practice hands separately, then sing the melody and play the left hand accompaniment.
Once you feel confident, you should try playing both hands together.

"Frankie and Johnny" has the typical 12 Bar Blues chord pattern:

4 bars of C; 2 bars of F; 2 bars of C; 1 bar of G; 1 bar of F and 2 bars of C.

If you learn this pattern you'll be all set to play many other famous 12 bar songs, such as "Rock Around the Clock," "In the Mood," "Kansas City," Ray Charles' music, early Elvis songs, like "Hound Dog" and "Jailhouse Rock," and many James Brown songs.

Audio examples can be found at CharlesSegal.com

ACCOMPANYING YOUR SINGING

If you prefer to sing instead of play the melodies, some of the patterns can be played with both hands. Follow the rhythmic pattern, but split the work between both hands: your left hand can play the bass notes and your right hand the chords. Below are some examples. **Audio examples can be found at CharlesSegal.com**

Each pattern lasts two bars.

TRANSPOSING ACCOMPANIMENT PATTERNS

Although all of the accompaniment examples are written for C chord, you'll notice that there are other chords in this book - F and G, for example. To use the patterns for other chords, you will need to "transpose" them. To quickly transpose the accompaniment patterns on pages 123-127 from the C chords to the F and G chords, follow these rules.

Let's use **pattern 5B** as an example:

Use the major scale diagrams on pages 143 and 144 to help you.

Start by figuring out which scale degree each note is in the key of C:

(i) The first note in the pattern is a C, which, of course, is the first note of the C major scale.

(ii) The second note is an E - the third note of the C major scale

(iii) The third note is a G - the fifth note of a C major scale.

(iv) The last note is an A - the sixth note of the C major scale.

Therefore the pattern is: 1 – 3 – 5 – 6

Now you can just match them up to a new scale. Let's take F major for example.

In the F major scale: 1 – 3 – 5 – 6 is F A C D

So, the same pattern in **F major** looks like this:

And in **G major**: 1 – 3 – 5 – 6 is G B D E and the pattern looks like this:

Although this may seem tricky at first, knowing how to transpose patterns into different keys is a very valuable tool for any pianist. So, take the time to study the patterns and play them in different keys. It may even be helpful to write them out yourself on a piece of staff paper.

Let's try ~~another~~ pattern 4A. Here's the pattern in the key of **C major**, with the scale degrees written below the notes to help you.

The same pattern in **F major** and **G major** would look like this:

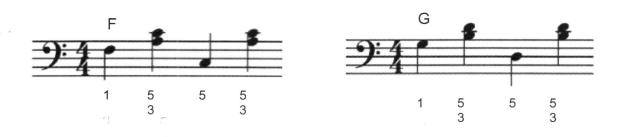

MORE TRANSPOSITION EXAMPLES

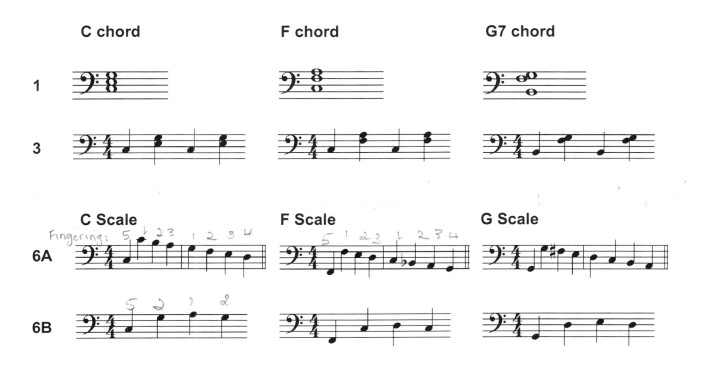

HOW TO GO ON FROM HERE

Congratulations!

You've conquered the most challenging parts of learning to play the keyboard – your mind and hands are used to playing and you can actually enjoy playing without being afraid of the instrument.

It's entirely up to you how you would like to proceed, but here are some suggestions:

You can continue to **play your favorite songs by ear**, using the techniques you learned at the beginning of this course and the accompaniment patterns.

You can move on to the **BONUS section** of this book, which is filled with more songs to practice as well as valuable resources for furthering your musical education.

You can buy the **music of other songs** and have fun playing those with the help of the **scale and chord charts** *on pages 142-150 of* the BONUS section of this book.

Even though you can **have fun and also impress your friends** with what you have learned up to now, you have really only scratched the surface of what you can achieve following the Instant method with very little effort.

If you want to accomplish more, you **can continue the Instant course**, where you can learn how to **play songs in different keys** and **expand your skills** in other ways, even learning **songwriting.**

Whatever you decide – we hope you had fun with **Instant Keyboard**.

We had fun showing you a new and painless way to play the keyboard.

You can contact us through our website: **www.CharlesSegal.com**

BONUS SECTION: ADDITIONAL SONGS TO PLAY

SONGS FOR OCCASIONS

It's gratifying to be able to sit down with friends and play a song for a happy occasion. Half the population of concert pianists will admit that unless they have the sheet music fully written out in front of them, they can't play "Happy Birthday" or any other song they haven't rehearsed.
So here's your chance to learn these by heart and outshine concert pianists!

"HAPPY BIRTHDAY"

Notice the waltz time signature (3/4) and the pick-up notes. The last three bars give you a chance to show off your chord inversions. You can play full chords for the C F C chords, then broken chords for G7 and C. Why don't you try a **running arpeggio** all the way up the keyboard for the last C chord? Play C broken chord in your left hand, then an octave higher with your right hand, then the next octave higher with the left hand and higher with the right hand, **all the way up the keyboard**. That should impress your friends!

"FOR HE'S A JOLLY GOOD FELLOW"

This is a very popular song amongst people of British descent.
So you can show off your "international style" by playing this song.
On the other hand – you could also play it as "The Bear Came Over the Mountain" and enjoy it just as much!

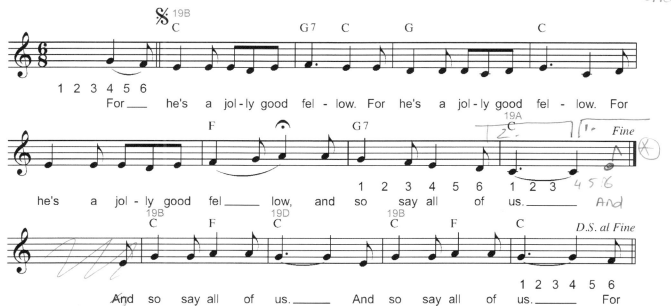

"WE WISH YOU A MERRY CHRISTMAS"

This is a happy sing-along where the title phrase pattern is
repeated three times, each time climbing to higher notes.
It will give you good practice at selecting convenient fingering.
Notice the first note is a pick-up note, starting on the count of "three".

"MY COUNTRY 'TIS OF THEE"

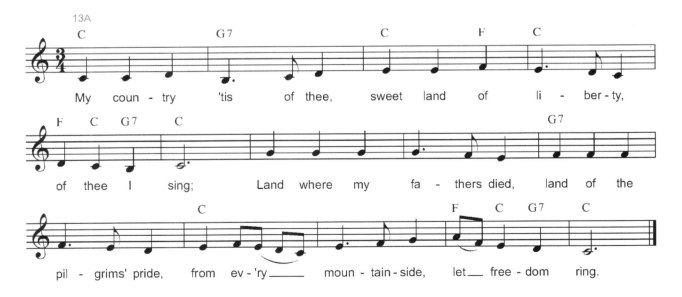

"I'VE BEEN WORKING ON THE RAILROAD"

There are lots of jumps in this song but the fingering suggestions will help.
Notice the C# accidental in the ninth bar. The timing has plenty of dotted notes
so you should count in "ands" from the first bar.

You're Not Alone

Music: Charles Segal
Lyrics: Barbara Brilliant
Available on iTunes.

2nd verse:

Somewhere a mother cries
Somewhere a lover weeps
Somewhere a baby fusses
and cannot get to sleep

How does one measure time
It's measured in love not years
Quality's in the giving
The truth is crystal clear

Go to CharlesSegal.com for audio examples!

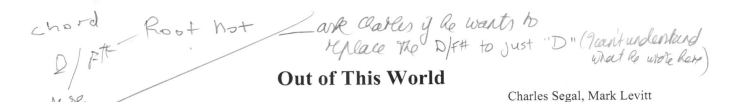

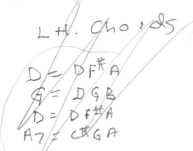

Jungle Rock 'n Roll

Music: Charles Segal
Lyrics: Shirley Peters
Available on iTunes.

O - cean to O-cean and na-tion to na - tion the whole pop-u - la - tion, finds con-so-la - tion, when
Tree-tops are creak-in', pyg-mies are peek-in, the lions roar a chor-us, dance mad-ly for us, the

Rock-in' 'n roll - in' they put their hearts and soul in, and guess where it got to now? Just
Monk-eys are play-ing, rhi - noc- e -ros are sway-ing and jum - bo starts swing-ing too Down

Lis - ten and you'll won - der a – bout that noise like thun-der, yes the jun-gle rocks 'n rolls. Right now the
Where the green is green-est no- ah's crea-tures are the keen-est, yes the jun-gle rocks 'n rolls.

Jung - gles in a ri - ot Where once was on-ly peace and qui - et. Now ev'ry

Gir – affe you'll find rock - in' And ev - 'ry hip - po you'll find roll – in'. The

Jungle Rock 'n Roll – page 2

MUSICAL SCALES

All scales in the same "family" follow the same pattern of notes.

The pattern for all Major scales is:

whole step, whole step, half step, whole step, whole step, whole step, half step

If you know this pattern than you can play any major scale!

For example, let's start with the key of C major:

(i) Start on middle C.
(ii) Now go one whole step up from C – the note is D.
(iii) A whole step up from D is E.
(iv) A half step up from E is F.
(v) A whole step up from F is G.
(vi) A whole step up from G is A.
(vii) A whole step up from A is B
(viii) A half step up from B is C.

The diagrams below illustrates the pattern of whole and half steps both on the Treble staff and on the keyboard.

```
  1     2     3     4     5     6     7     1
whole whole half  whole whole whole  half
```

```
 C  D  E  F  G  A  B  C
 W  W  H  W  W  W  H
```

142 © 2011 Charles Segal Publications, 16 Grace Rd. Ste 1, Newton, MA 02459

Now that you know the pattern of whole and half steps, try playing an **F major scale** on your own, without looking at the diagram below. *Hint:* there is one black key in this scale.

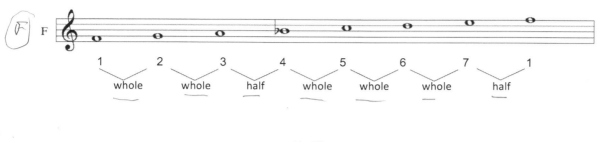

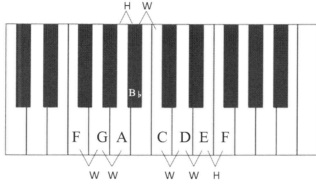

Now try playing a **G major scale** using the pattern of whole and half steps. *Hint:* there is one black key in this scale.

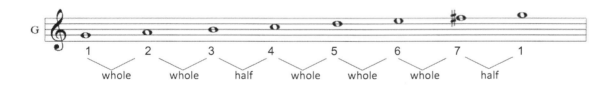

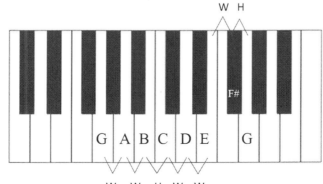

Challenge: Play Major scales in all the twelve different keys. See page 144 and 145 for guidance.
Ultimate challenge: Practise one new scale each week

MAJOR SCALES AND KEY SIGNATURE CHART

TIP: When playing scales avoid playing the black keys with your thumb.

LH = Left hand fingering   RH = Right hand fingering

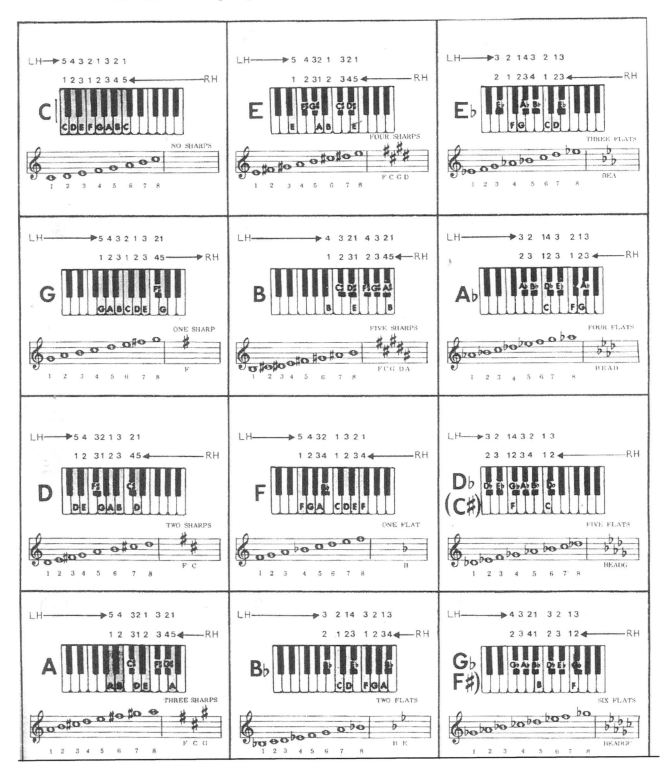

MAJOR SCALES
There are 12 major keys.

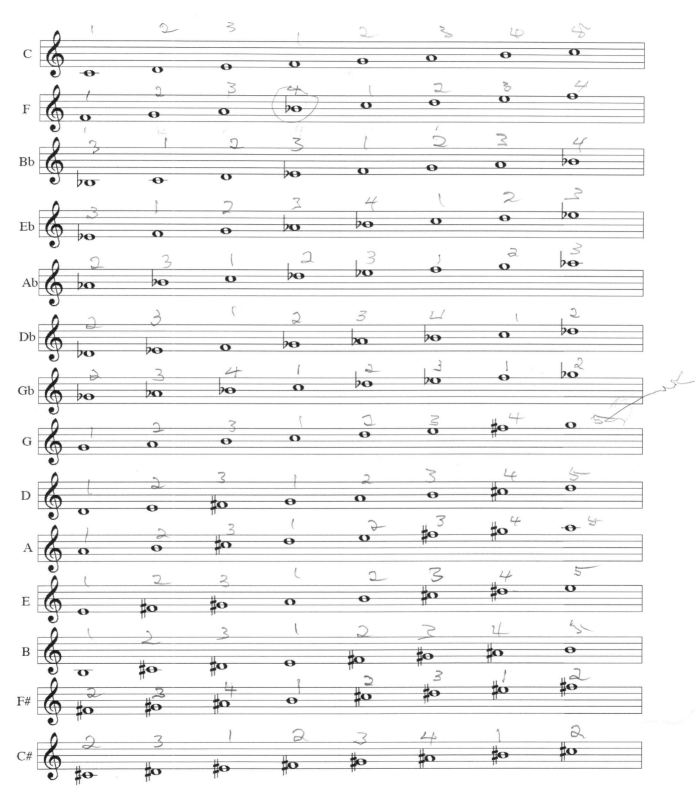

You will notice that there are 14 scales listed above this is because D♭ and C# and G♭ and F# are enharmonic. *For a reminder about enharmonic notes see page 95.*

NATURAL MINOR SCALES
The finger numbers are for the right hand.

HARMONIC MINOR SCALES

Harmonic Minor scales are the same as Natural Minor scales except:
the 7th note of the Harmonic Minor scale is raised one half step.
For example, in an "A" Natural Minor scale the 7th note is a G but in the Harmonic Minor the 7th note is a G#.

BLUES SCALES

The Blues scale only has 6 notes and can be formed from any
Major Scale by playing the **1, flat 3, 4, sharp 4, 5, flat 7**
For example, a C Major scale is **C D E F G A B C**
and the C Blues scale is **C Eb F F# G Bb C**
To play a **Pentatonic scale** simply leave out the 4th note of the Blues scale!

The Blues and Pentatonic scales are commonly used for Jazz,
Blues and Rock n' Roll and is a helpful tool for improvisation.
Practice the scales below and experiment playing them against various major and minor chords.

148

go Back to page 121.

CHORD CHART

	C	G	D	A	E	B
MAJOR	C 5 2 1 G C E	G 5 3 1 G B D	D 5 3 1 F♯A D	A 4 2 1 A C♯E	E 5 3 1 G♯B E	B 5 2 1 F♯ B D♯
MINOR	Cm 5 2 1 G C E♭	Gm 5 3 1 G B♭ D	Dm 5 2 1 A D F	Am 4 2 1 A C E	Em 5 3 1 G B E	Bm 5 2 1 F♯ B D
7th	C7 5 3 2 1 G B♭ C E	G7 5 3 2 1 G B D F	D7 5 3 21 F♯ A C D	A7 54 2 1 GA C♯ E	E7 5 3 21 G♯B DE	B7 5 32 1 F♯AB D♯
(O) DIM Diminished	Cdim 5 3 2 1 G♭A C E♭	Gdim 5 3 2 1 G B♭D♭E	Ddim 5 3 2 1 G♯ B D F	Adim 5 3 2 1 G♭A C E♭	Edim 5 3 2 1 G B♭ D♭E	Bdim 5 3 2 1 F A♭B D
MAJOR 7th	Cmaj7 5 3 2 1 C E G B	Gmaj7 5 3 2 1 G B D F♯	Dmaj7 5 3 2 1 D F♯A C♯	Amaj7 5 3 2 1 A C♯E G♯	Emaj7 5 3 2 1 E G♯B D♯	Bmaj7 5 3 2 1 B D♯ F♯ A
MINOR 7th	Cm 7 5 3 2 1 G B♭ C E♭	Gm 7 5 3 2 1 G B♭ D F	Dm 7 5 32 1 A CD F	Am 7 54 2 1 GA C E	Em 7 5 3 21 G B DE	Bm 7 5 32 1 F♯A B D
+ AUG AUGMENTED	C+ 4 2 1 G♯ C E	G+ 5 3 1 G B D♯	D+ 5 3 1 F♯ A♯ D	A+ 4 2 1 A C♯ F	E+ 4 2 1 G♯ C E	B+ 4 2 1 G B D♯
MAJOR 6th	C6 54 2 1 G A C E	G6 5 3 21 G B DE	D6 5 32 1 F♯A B D	A6 5 3 21 F♯ A C♯E	E6 5 3 2 1 G♯B C♯E	B6 54 2 1 F♯G♯B D♯
9th	C9 5 3 21 G B♭ DE	G9 54 2 1 AB D F	D9 5 3 2 1 F♯A C E	A9 5 3 2 1 G B C♯E	E9 54 2 1 F♯G♯B D	B9 5 3 21 F♯A C♯D♯

Please Note (go Back to page 121.
To join the sounds I've used
Inversions you don't have to start on the
Root note F maj. chord Root is F. I started
F A C — A C F.

Chord Chart

	F	B♭	E♭	A♭	D♭(C#)	G♭(F#)
MAJOR	F (A C F)	B♭ (B♭ D F)	E♭ (G B♭ E♭)	A♭ (A♭ C E♭)	D♭ (A♭ D♭ F)	F#(G♭) (F# A# C#)
MINOR	Fm (A♭ C F)	B♭m (B♭ D♭ F)	E♭m (G♭ B♭ E♭)	A♭m (A♭ B E♭)	D♭m (A♭ D♭ E)	F#(G♭)m (F# A C#)
7th	F7 (A C E♭ F)	B♭7 (F A♭ B♭ D)	E♭7 (G B♭ D♭ E♭)	A♭7 (G♭ A♭ C E♭)	D♭7 (A♭ B D♭ F)	F#(G♭)7 (F# A# C# E)
(O) DIM Diminished	Fdim (F A♭ B D)	B♭dim (G B♭ D♭ E)	E♭dim (G♭ A C E♭)	A♭dim (F A♭ B D)	D♭dim (G B♭ D♭ E)	F#(G♭)dim (F# A C E♭)
MAJOR 7th	Fmaj7 (F A C E)	B♭maj7 (B♭ D F A)	E♭maj7 (E♭ G B♭ D)	A♭maj7 (A♭ C E♭ G)	D♭maj7 (D♭ F A♭ C)	F#(G♭)maj7 (F# A# C# F)
MINOR 7th	Fm7 (A♭ C E♭ F)	B♭m7 (A♭ B♭ D♭ F)	E♭m7 (G♭ B♭ D♭ E♭)	A♭m7 (G♭ A♭ B E♭)	D♭m7 (A♭ B D♭ E)	F#(G♭)m7 (F# A C# E)
+ AUG AUGMENTED	F+ (A C# F)	B♭+ (G♭ B♭ D)	E♭+ (G B E♭)	A♭+ (A♭ C E)	D♭+ (A D♭ F)	F#(G♭)+ (F# A# D)
MAJOR 6th	F6 (A C D F)	B♭6 (G B♭ D)	E♭6 (G B♭ C E♭)	A♭6 (A♭ C E♭ F)	D♭6 (A♭ B♭ D♭ F)	F#(G♭)6 (F# A# C# D#)
9th	F9 (G A C E♭)	B♭9 (F A♭ C D)	E♭9 (G B♭ D♭ F)	A♭9 (G♭ B♭ C E♭)	D♭9 (A♭ B E♭ F)	F#(G♭)9 (G# A# C# E)

CIRCLE OF FIFTHS

The Circle of Fifths shows the 12 key signatures and the relationship between minor and major keys.
Use this chart to help you easily identify key signatures.
The grey, lower case letters are the relative minors of the capitalized major keys.
For example, a key signature with no sharps or flats denotes both "C major" and "a minor" keys.

Use this acronym to help you remember the correct order of placing sharps and flats in a Key Signature.
Order of sharps: **F**ather **C**harles **G**oes **D**own **A**nd **E**nds **B**attle
Order of flats: **B**attle **E**nds **A**nd **D**own **G**oes **C**harles' **F**ather

There are many other interesting uses for the Circle of Fifths that you will learn as you advance in your musical knowledge.

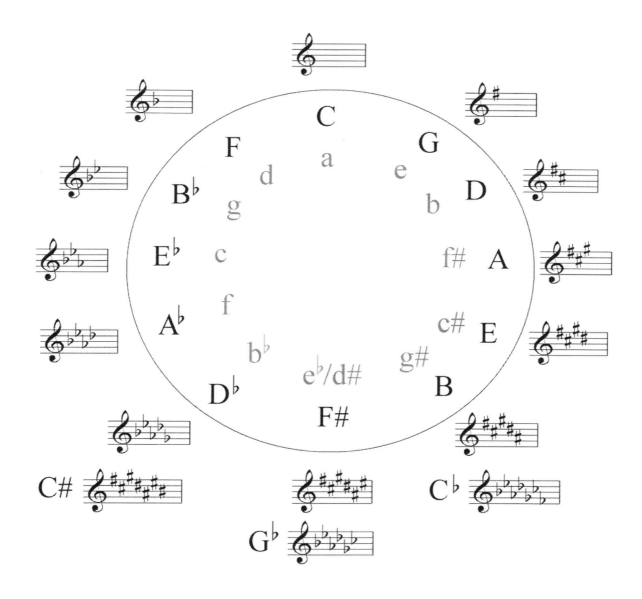

© 2011 Charles Segal Publications, 16 Grace Rd. Ste 1, Newton, MA 02459

CHORD SYMBOLS

There is more than one way to write most chord symbols. This chart lists the most common. When writing your own music we suggest using the chord symbols that appear first in each row, as these are the most widely recognized symbols.

Examples are given in the key of C.

[handwritten: Chord is a Ⓒ]
[handwritten: Cmaj7 = 1 3 5 7]

TRIADS

[handwritten: 1 3 5 / C E G]

Major	C, Cmaj, C△, CM
Minor	Cm, C-, Cmi, Cmin *[= Cm 1 ♭3 5]*
Augmented	C+, Caug *[= C+ = 1 3 ♯5]*
Diminished	C°, Cdim *[Cdim = 1 ♭3 ♭5 6]*

7th CHORDS

[handwritten: Its not a Triad its 4 notes C E G B 1 3 5 7]

Major 7	Cmaj7, C△7, CM7
Minor 7	Cm7, C-7, Cmi7, Cmin7
Augmented 7	C+7, Caug7 *[= C+7 = 1 3 ♯5 7]*
Diminished 7	C°7, Cdim7 *[= C E♭ F♯ A 1 ♭3 ♭5 6]*
Dominant 7	C7, Cdom7 *[C7 = C E G B♭]*
Minor Major 7	C-maj7, C-△7 *[Cm maj7 = C E♭ G B 1 ♭3 5 7]*
Half Diminished	Cø7, C-7♭5, Cmi7♭5 *[Cm7♭5 = 1 ♭3 5 ♭7]*

Made in the USA
Charleston, SC
01 August 2011